Sketch & Paint Techniques

PORTRAITS & THE FIGURE

ROGER COLEMAN · JAMES HORTON

DIAMOND BOOKS

This edition published 1995 by Diamond Books
77–85 Fulham Palace Road
Hammersmith, London W6 8JB

First published as two volumes:

Learn to Paint Portraits © Roger Coleman, 1988
Edited by Josephine Christian
Photography by Ben Bennett and Nigel Cheffers-Heard

Learn to Draw the Figure © James Horton 1985, 1986
Photography by Peter Lofts

Designed by Caroline Hill

ISBN 0 261 66542 1

Printed in Italy

CONTENTS

PORTRAITS

Roger Coleman

PORTRAIT OF AN ARTIST
ROGER COLEMAN

Roger Coleman was born in 1930, in an industrial village near Leicester. He studied painting at Leicester College of Art from 1948 to 1951, and it was during this time that he became particularly interested in portrait painting. In 1952, while he was doing his National Service with the Royal Artillery, he won a national portrait painting competition.

After National Service he spent four years studying at the Royal College of Art, and became editor of the college journal, *Ark*. When he left college he joined the staff of *Design* magazine as an assistant editor. He spent the next few years working for *Design*, writing and broadcasting on art, design and television, and, as a member of the exhibitions committee at the Institute of Contemporary Arts, organizing art exhibitions. He did very little painting during this period. In 1959 he returned to painting

and he also started to do illustrations, mostly for news magazines. During the 1960s he achieved a world-wide reputation as an illustrator.

It was in the early seventies that he moved from London to the village of Burpham, near Arundel, on the Sussex Downs, where he now lives with his wife and two daughters. Since then he has devoted almost all his working time to painting. His works include landscapes and sporting pictures – and hundreds of portraits, mostly of his family and friends. In 1980 *Downland*, a book of Roger Coleman's paintings of Burpham, its characters and its surroundings, was published by the Viking Press.

BELOW **Fig. 1** Roger Coleman working in his studio

OPPOSITE **Fig. 2** *Self-portrait* 1979 oil on canvas
40 × 40 cm/16 × 16 in

WHY PAINT PORTRAITS?

Until about the middle of the last century, most paintings were commissioned from the artist as a job of work. A painting would be done to a pre-agreed specification and with a particular application in mind: notions of self-expression, today regarded as the artist's true province, came a lot lower on the scale of priorities – if they appeared on it at all.

Portraits, especially those of the great and powerful, were positively hemmed around with specifications. The political implications of the likenesses of popes, emperors, generals and their kind were at least as significant as the artistic aspects. The portrait of a king was intended to symbolize his kingship rather than to disclose his character as a human being. Indeed, often the actual, physical appearance was modified to provide whatever regal attributes were held desirable. For example, there is a portrait of the Spanish King Philip IV by Velazquez, one of the greatest of all portrait painters, which was entirely repainted, some five years after its completion, precisely along these lines. X-ray photographs have revealed, in the first portrait, an altogether less glamorous individual – shorter in the neck, double-chinned and larger round the waist – a much less convincing candidate for the divine right of kings.

In the eighteenth century the numbers of those eligible, as it were, to have their portraits painted increased enormously; in England and Scotland this period was the high point in portraiture – think of all the stately homes lined with family portraits. With the exception of Turner and Constable, all the most famous British artists of this period were, professionally speaking, portrait painters: Reynolds, Gainsborough, Ramsay, Raeburn, Romney, Lawrence, among them. Whatever other kinds of painting these artists aspired to, their bread and butter came from painting the faces of, now, not only royalty and the aristocracy but also members of the new, rising middle classes – farmers, landowners and brewers, as well as actors, writers and people from the more raffish reaches of society.

Gainsborough complained in his letters of the need to paint faces all the time, when what he really wanted to do was to get out into the country, make music and paint landscapes. Similar feeling was expressed by John Singer Sargent at the end of the nineteenth century. Sargent, anachronistically, was the last of the great professional portrait painters in the sense that Gainsborough and Lawrence were professionals. By his time, the tradition that had enabled Gainsborough and Raeburn to paint bread-and-butter portraits that were at the same time great paintings was almost exhausted. In the twentieth century most of the best portraits have been painted by artists who are not professional portrait painters, painting people (often family or friends) not to fulfil a commission, but because they want to paint them. Picasso, Walter Sickert and Wyndham Lewis, for example, all professional painters but certainly not professional portrait painters, produced some wonderful portraits. On the other hand, professional, commissioned portrait painting now often tends to result in images that are vapid and bland.

Some years ago John Rothenstein, talking of Augustus John, spoke of how in the past an artist was sustained by a workmanlike and dignified tradition; and how the waning of this tradition had left the present-day portrait painter face to face with his sitter, dependent, as his predecessors were not, on his *personal* response to the face in front of him. Which is the position of us all, professional and amateur alike. Today the answer to the question, 'Why paint portraits?' is simply, 'Because I want to do it'. Because painting a portrait is very, very interesting, to the painter and to the sitter.

Having just implied that you can follow your feelings when you paint, I shall now tell you that you should do no such thing. When I say that I paint portraits for pleasure – and I do, I seldom paint portraits professionally, I almost always do them just because I want to – I do not mean that there are no guidelines or constraints.

The basic minimum requirement of a portrait is that it should look like its subject. This is all very well as long as we do not inquire too closely into what we mean by 'like'. We all know what we think we mean; but to paint a likeness we have to be a bit clearer. First, it helps if you know the kind of thing you want to achieve: what kind of likeness do you want? In the case of the Velazquez portrait mentioned earlier, the first, painted-over version was 'like' the man, whereas the second could be said to be more 'like' the king, and, since the enhancement of majesty was one of the painter's obligations, you could argue that the second was a more satisfactory likeness than the first.

However, nowadays when people speak of a portrait being 'like' its subject, they will most probably be thinking in terms of a photographic likeness. But it would be wrong, certainly from the painter's point

Fig. 3 *Jack Lloyd* 1979 watercolour portrait painted for *Downland* 38 × 56 cm/15 × 22 in

of view, to regard the camera as providing an absolute standard by which the look of things can be understood. The camera is a wonderful recording instrument, but it does distort: insidiously, since people seldom appreciate that it does, or at least the ways in which it does. 'As good as a photograph', people comment, when they wish to compliment an artist on the fidelity of his rendering of, say, his wife's features. Later in this book (pages 40–43) I shall deal in more detail with the way a painter can use photography, and with some of the problems that can arise from too enthusiastic an acceptance of its convenience.

There are many examples of impressive photographic portraits, taken by perceptive, talented and skilled photographers. Great photographers have produced photographic portraits that are great works of art. But in the last analysis the camera records its print impersonally, and surely a portrait ought to be more than that: should it not be a human reaction to a human being? But if so, is not the painter then primarily concerned with something beyond, or underlying, the facts? The practical answer to this second question is no. A portrait painter is concerned with the facts, you might argue exclusively so, and a good portrait has to treat seriously the shape, proportions, texture and colour of the sitter's face, observing them closely and measuring them carefully. But what about the character of the sitter, the psychology, is not that what portraits are about?

What you can say with confidence is that there are painters (Rembrandt comes to mind, Holbein and Velazquez too) whose portraits tempt one to psychological, even spiritual speculations; there are also portraits which you feel are profound assessments of a personality, even though you do not know that personality. At the other end of the scale there are portraits that are technically quite competent but nonetheless shallow and inert.

But however much you use words like 'insight' or 'perception' to explain the effects of a likeness, the painter must concern himself most with physical problems such as proportion, application of paint, composition and colour, and get them in the right combination to make a good picture.

Whether or not Rembrandt consciously, as it were, employed the spiritual insight credited to him when he was painting, I do not know, but I rather doubt it. The demonstration of feelings, emotions and attitudes, any sort of 'interpretation', in fact, other than the most general, practically unconscious sort, does not help, and stands a good chance of hindering, the creation of any kind of a portrait. Any artist will have his work cut out simply translating the way the model appears to him into paint on canvas, without adding the difficulties of character analysis. It is equally unprofitable to consider the 'meaning' of the sitter's features, which do not constitute an index of human characteristics – for example, to equate high foreheads with nobility and cling to notions about close-set eyes, mean mouths, and, as my grandmother used to, criminal ears.

The depth we perceive in great portraits seems to arise, almost without the conscious participation of the painter, from the physical process of making the picture, not from his psychological speculations. Of course, in the situation of most amateur portrait painters such speculations will hardly be invited, since, unlike the professional, they will not be meeting the sitter for the first time at the first sitting. Amateurs (and I count myself as a portrait amateur, although a professional painter) usually paint family or close friends, and will therefore be free from the temptation to read all sorts of traits in, and project all sorts of characteristics on, the friendly features facing them.

All they have to do is paint.

9

EQUIPMENT

I have always felt that it is an error to make a mystique out of your equipment, buying it for its own sake, or because it looks nice, which it can. Start with the basic essentials and add to them if you need to. Obviously, if you are starting from scratch you will need guidance from some source: the following recommendations are not the results of exhaustive tests, but I think they are as sound as any.

I can only recommend what I use myself, so I shall go through the mediums I use, giving my suggestions.

I draw in pen and ink (which includes fibre-tipped pens), pencil and charcoal, and paint in oil, watercolour and pastel, and very, very occasionally in acrylic.

Pen and ink

The pen I use most of the time is a mapping pen. Some people find that mapping pens are a bit fine, and do not produce a strong enough line; but since my pen drawings are usually not very large, this does not worry me. What I do like about mapping pens is their flexibility, the way they respond to changes in pressure, producing lines of different strength and character. I use a black Indian ink, such as Daler-Rowney's Kandahar, and, on odd occasions, brown or sepia (of course, waterproof inks come in the basic colours should you need them).

Fibre-tipped pens are available in a wide range of thicknesses, from very broad indeed to extremely fine. Again, as most of my drawings are small, I generally prefer a fine one.

Pencil

Pencils are graded in degrees of hardness, from 6H, the hardest, to 6B, the softest, with HB at the mid-point. The H grades are intended largely for technical drawing. Hardness and softness are relative notions, certainly relative to the surface they are used on – a line with an HB on, say, brick or plaster will seem soft, as a line in 2B on glossy paper will seem hard. It is not necessary to buy a whole range of pencils: start with HB, B and 2B and add if you need to. I use a 2B for most pencil drawings, though I sometimes use a softer grade if I am doing a drawing with a lot of dark tone in it. 2B is also about the right weight for pencil indications at the beginning of a watercolour – soft enough not to dent the paper,

which would show when the wash was laid, but sufficiently hard not to make dirty marks.

Charcoal

I use charcoal both as a drawing medium in its own right and as a means of indicating the basic proportions on a canvas before starting to paint.

Charcoal comes boxed in three weights – thin, medium and large. I use thin and medium sticks. You will need to fix charcoal drawings, using a special charcoal fixative. This is available either in a bottle with a blow-spray or conveniently packaged in an aerosol. You will also need a soft putty rubber, which will erase charcoal marks cleanly.

Oil paints

Artists' colourmen produce enormous ranges of colours in oil paint. Daler-Rowney, for example, have a list of eighty-eight colours. Some of these will be 'fugitive' (that is, subject to fading and alterations) and others only 'moderately permanent'. On the other hand, very few artists use more than a dozen or so. The aim should always be to use as few as you can. Titian, it is said, used nine, and Rubens, fourteen.

On occasions I have used as few as five (Titanium White, Cadmium Lemon, Cadmium Red, French Ultramarine and Ivory Black), but I generally select from about nine to a dozen. Subject-matter will affect your choice of colours to some extent, but the following list should enable you to tackle most things: Titanium White, Cadmium Lemon, Cadmium Yellow, Yellow Ochre, Raw Sienna, Burnt Umber, Indian Red, Cadmium Red, Crimson Alizarin, French Ultramarine, Cadmium Green and Ivory Black. To this list you could add two blues, a phthalo blue, such as Monestial Blue, and Cerulean or Coeruleum (the spelling is immaterial), a very light blue useful for cooling flesh tints. Some people find Viridian an indispensable green and Cobalt Blue an indispensable blue – I do not.

Be wary of Indian Red, Crimson Alizarin and the phthalo blues: they are all very dominant colours, and can easily saturate your mixtures if you are not careful.

All colours are available in two qualities, Artists' and Students'. Artists' are finer in quality and consequently more expensive.

Fig. 4 Basic equipment for drawing and oils

Key

1 Aerosol fixative
2 Linseed oil
3 Drying medium
4 Retouching varnish
5 White spirit
6 Brushes for oil painting
7 Rag
8 Oil paints
9 Wax varnish
10 Palette
11 Dippers
12 Gel medium
13 Oil painting knife
14 Palette knife
15 Charcoal
16 Putty rubber
17 Fixative
18 Spray diffuser
19 Pencils
20 Indian ink
21 Mapping pens
22 Fibre-tipped pen
23 Sketchbook

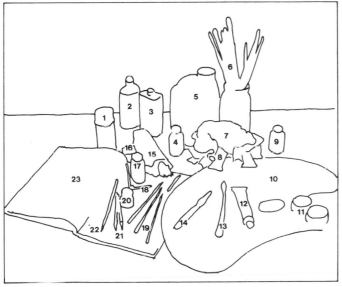

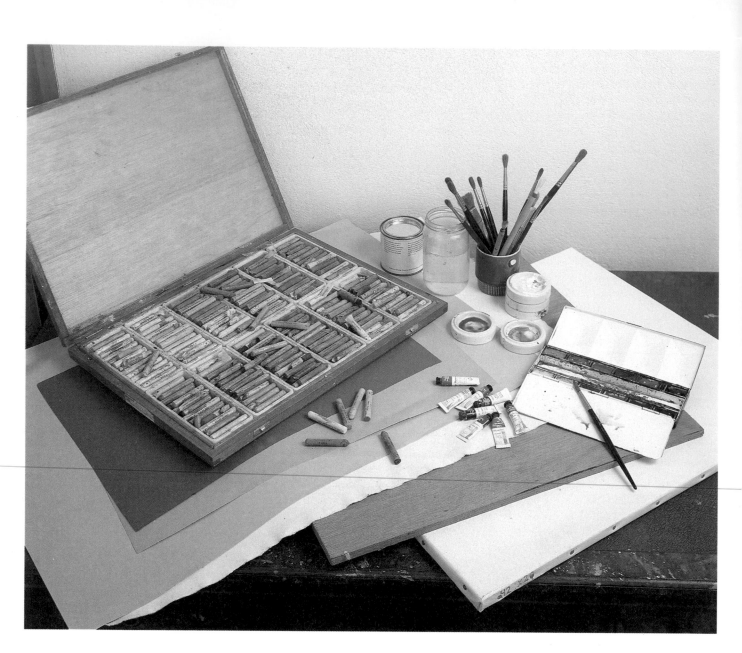

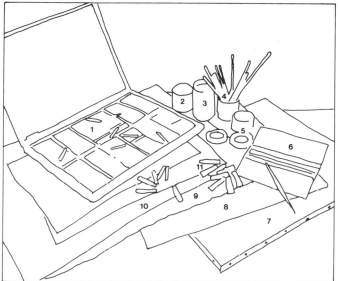

Fig. 5 Basic equipment for watercolours and pastels

Key

1 Box of pastels
2 Acrylic 'gesso' primer
3 Water jar
4 Watercolour brushes
5 Ceramic palettes
6 Watercolour box
7 Canvas
8 Plywood
9 Watercolour paper
10 Coloured pastel paper
11 Tubes of watercolour paint

For years I diluted oil paint with a mixture of linseed oil and turpentine – more turpentine than oil. But recently I have used a gel drying medium. As a student I was always taught to avoid drying agents of any kind, but manufacturers claim that the new ones based on synthetic resin are free from vices. If you have no need to speed up the drying time of your paint, don't take any risks, stick to the oil and turpentine mixture.

Watercolours

Watercolours are available in pans, half-pans (the usual components of a watercolour box) and tubes. I prefer tubes, which I squeeze into the pans of a watercolour box. You can get boxes containing almost any number of half-pans. I have several boxes, but the one I use most of the time contains twelve whole pans in which I put out the following colours: Aureolin, Cadmium Yellow, Yellow Ochre, Raw Sienna, Raw Umber, Burnt Umber, Cadmium Red, Crimson Alizarin, Coeruleum, French Ultramarine, Monestial Blue and Oxide of Chromium. To this list of colours you could add Ivory Black (it is seldom you will need black in watercolour), Cadmium Lemon and Light Red. This selection is an all-purpose one suitable for most subjects.

When the need arises I use white gouache mixed with watercolour to give a less transparent pigment. Sometimes the need is simply to retouch small details. At other times it may be necessary to cover substantial areas with opaque paint.

Pastels

You can buy pastels in different-sized boxes. Daler-Rowney's boxes range from a basic set containing twelve assorted colours right up to 144. There is a useful box containing thirty-six sticks which should provide the beginner with a large enough range to see whether the medium appeals or not. You can also buy the colours individually: there are over 190 tints to choose from in the Daler-Rowney range.

You will also need a fixative, of the type used for fixing charcoal drawings (see page 10).

Acrylics

With acrylics, as with all mediums, your choice of colours should be guided by simplicity. Mine would be Cadmium Yellow, Yellow Ochre, Raw Sienna, Venetian Red, Cadmium Red, Permanent Rose, Ultramarine, Monestial Blue, Bright Green, black and white. As well as the colours, you can get supporting products such as retarder to hold back the drying time, and texture paste to give the paint body.

Brushes

There are two general rules about brushes. The first is to buy the best you can afford. The second is always to use one size larger than the size you first thought of.

Hog-hair brushes are, for all but the smallest paintings, quite the best means of applying oil paint. Of the various shapes you can obtain I use just two, the round and the filbert shapes. I avoid square-ended brushes and have always urged students away from them, as I think they can easily lead to mannered ways of applying paint.

For watercolour painting, pure sable brushes are the best. They are also very expensive, but they do come in different grades priced accordingly. Brushes made of ox-hair or a mixture of ox-hair and sable can also be used for watercolours. Numbers 5, 6 and 7 are the most useful brush sizes, and even a number 7 brush, if it is a good one, will be quite suitable for detailed work.

Then there are the synthetic brushes which are advertised as being suitable for watercolours, oil paints and acrylics. My own experience, using them for oil paints, has been less than satisfactory, but I know people who use nothing else.

In the end, use the brushes that you like using and feel comfortable with, no matter what the experts tell you – providing, of course, that you also feel happy with the results.

Supports

The traditional support for oil paintings is, of course, canvas, which is a joy to use and is very light in weight – a consideration if you paint large pictures. It is expensive, though.

Hardboard can be used – the smooth side, not the textured side, which has far too aggressive a pattern, and plywood is a particular favourite of mine. Less usual, perhaps, but a very satisfactory surface for oil painting, is paper; it needs to be fairly thick, certainly not less than 290 gsm (140 lb) in weight (see page 14). Any surface to be used for oil painting must be primed either with size or with an acrylic primer. There are many traditional recipes for primers, but nowadays most people use acrylic gesso.

Paper for watercolours are very much a matter of individual choice. Finding one you like can involve a lot of trial and error. Watercolour paper is made in three surfaces, Rough, HP (hot pressed) and Not (not hot pressed): the Rough, quite reasonably, is rough and the HP is smooth, with the Not somewhere in between. I use a Not paper most of the time, and this is the surface I would recommend to anyone beginning watercolour painting.

Watercolour paper is graded by weight, stated either in grams per square metre or as the weight of a ream in pounds. Obviously, the thicker the paper the heavier it is. The weights of paper generally used for watercolours range from about 150 gsm (72 lb) to 425 gsm (200 lb).

The thinner papers need to be stretched before use, or they will cockle. To stretch a piece of paper, first wet it thoroughly, then fasten it to a drawing board using strips of gummed paper (not sticky tape). The paper will dry taut and flat. However, I don't like stretching paper myself – it makes me nervous, and the time taken doing it acts as a constraint. Watercolour is a medium that profits from boldness, and I want to feel able to use the paint freely and confidently. So I always use a paper heavy enough not to cockle when the water is put on, that is, with a minimum weight of 290 gsm (140 lb). For water-colour white paper is almost always preferable to tinted.

Acrylic can be worked on virtually any support or surface, from raw canvas to paper. Since acrylic is a plastic paint it will not crack, as oil paint can, so a firm support is not functionally necessary. Again un-like oil paint, it does no damage to the support, so no priming is necessary on that score. However, acrylic gesso provides a pleasant surface to work on and cuts down the 'tooth' of canvas.

Pastel, too, can be applied to any surface. It is best, though, to avoid the extremes of roughness and smoothness. A support with too assertive a tooth makes the soft pigment sticks difficult to handle. And at the opposite pole a very smooth paper can also lead to difficulties, as the pastel may clog the paper's texture too quickly.

Other equipment

You will also need a drawing board (a good size is half-imperial – 38 × 56 cm/15 × 22 in), a sketchbook and a palette knife. And you will need an easel. You can hold a drawing board with one hand and draw with the other, but you can't paint like that; the canvas, or whatever, must be held firmly so that it remains in constant relationship to your subject. There are several kinds of easel to choose from – sketching ones that fold up, radial easels such as you find in art schools, and the table-top variety.

Fig. 6 Easels in the artist's studio. From left to right: radial easel, studio easel, watercolour easel with drawing board

ANATOMY

All artists concerned with the human figure should have some knowledge of anatomy. They should have an idea of how the body is constructed, how it articulates, and the manner in which the parts under the skin give rise to the bumps and concavities on the surface. Such knowledge is a great help in realizing more clearly the figure you are painting. Here I am limiting a vast and intensely interesting subject to a brief study of the skull and its muscles as they immediately affect the portrait painter. However, I would urge students who seriously want to draw or paint the figure to enlarge on these notes for themselves, by consulting one of the many books that deal with anatomy for artists.

The bones, of course, are the support of the body – its structure. While their shape cannot be seen directly, they affect appearance more than one might at first imagine. They are not uniformly covered with muscle, and there are significant parts of the body where the bones are close to the surface of the skin: the knuckles are an obvious example; so, more importantly in our case, is the skull. Where bones are close to the surface you get clear and well-defined highlights, as the skin is smoother and tighter than in areas where the bone is deep or where the muscle hangs away from it.

The bones of the head

Fig. 7 shows front and side views of a skull, with the principal bones marked. A portrait painter will find that the following points, particularly, are worth keeping in mind.

Only about half the nose is bone: the lower part, which is the most variable and characteristic, consists of cartilage.

The white and iris of the eye are simply the parts of the eyeball which show: the remainder is located behind the rim of the eye socket. Always try to sense where the rim is on your subject – often, particularly with thin people, it is easy to see. The part of the eye surround that 'bags' with age, which is muscle, can overlap the rim at its bottom edge.

It is very clear from a plan view that the teeth are arranged in a sort of arc. Students who fail to appreciate this tend to draw them flat on to the front of the face, looking a bit like a car's radiator grill (not even the two upper front teeth are flat). Remember, the top teeth usually, though not always, overlap the bottom ones.

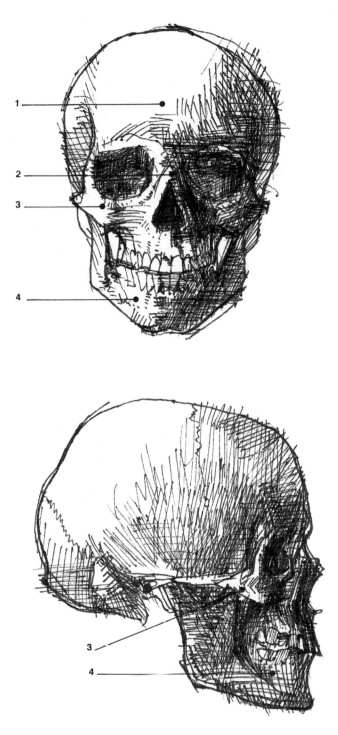

Fig. 7 The bones of the skull, front and side views
1 Frontal bone   3 Zygomatic arch
2 Nasal bone   4 Mandible

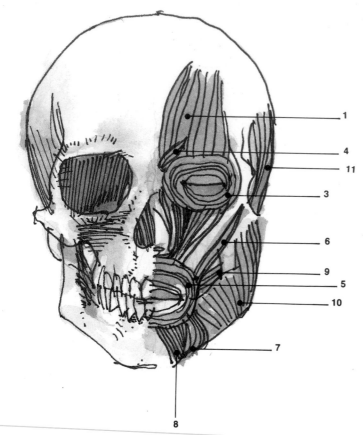

Fig. 8 The muscles of the head, front and side views

MUSCLES OF THE SCALP

1 **Frontalis:** covers the forehead, reaching from above the eyes to the galea (the tendon-like sheath that covers the skull), and moves the galea and the skin of the forehead
2 **Occipitalis:** located at the lower back of the head (invisible except in the bald), it moves the galea backwards

MUSCLES OF THE FACE

3 **Orbicularis oculi:** covering the eye socket and eyeball, including the eyelids, its function is to open and close the eye
4 **Corrugator:** draws the eyebrows towards each other, in frowning
5 **Orbicularis oris:** encircling the mouth, it is used in opening and closing the mouth and in pursing the lips
6 **Zygomaticus major:** pulls the mouth upwards, as in smiling
7 **Depressor anguli oris:** pulls the mouth down
8 **Depressor labii inferioris:** pulls the lower lip down
9 **Buccinator:** the muscle used when you blow
10 **Masseter:** a strongly defined muscle, it closes the mouth, as in chewing
11 **Temporalis:** fills the temple and attaches to the lower jaw behind the zygomatic arch: a chewing muscle

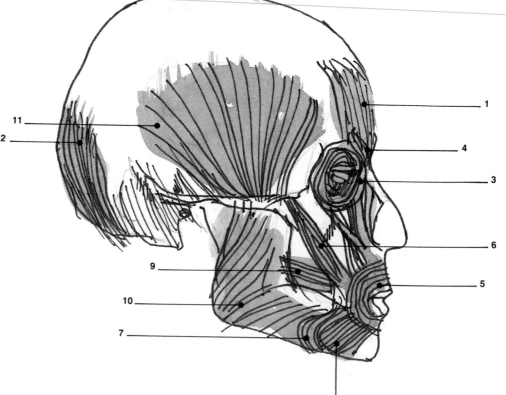

The muscles of the head

The principal muscles of the head are marked in **fig. 8**. It is important to understand what they do and the direction in which their fibres run, as this affects the surface appearance.

16

LIGHT

Light often provides the motivation for a painter. Frequently, I will start to paint a portrait because I have been struck, not so much by the face of the subject, as by the way light happens to fall on the cheekbone, or the nose.

But many amateur painters will set up a still-life or a portrait in a way which shows a lack of awareness of how the light is behaving. A painter may want to paint something because he feels that it has a beautiful shape or colour, and fail to realize that the shape can be obliterated by bad lighting, and the colour adulterated by unwanted reflections.

Much of the character of a portrait resides in the way light is used. Most Old Master portraits are lit very simply, with the head light against a dark background. This approach not only concentrates attention on the head, but also makes it easier to relate the details of the features to the head as a whole. The light itself generally comes from a single source, three-quarters on to the face and well above the sitter's head. The effect of this is to illuminate the front of the head and to confine the significant area of tone to one side or the other. The head has a light side and a dark side. The sketches after Velazquez in **figs. 9** and **10** show how this works. It is dramatic lighting, and it simplifies complex areas, such as that around the eye and the eye socket. It brings closer the tones of iris and pupil and completes the description of shape with a single highlight.

Rembrandt used light in the same basic way, but exaggerating it for even more dramatic effect. He

BELOW LEFT **Fig. 9** A sketch based on a portrait by Velazquez
ABOVE **Fig. 10** A sketch based on a portrait by Velazquez
BELOW **Fig. 11** A sketch based on a self-portrait by Rembrandt

Fig. 12 *George
Gent* 1978
watercolour portrait
painted for
Downland
38 × 56 cm/
15 × 22 in

would pose the sitter, often himself, so that the face seems to be turning either away from or towards the light (see **fig. 11**). Sometimes the eyes are half-concealed in deep patches of shadow, with forehead, nose and cheekbone illuminated.

The light we see in Old Master portraits is not the light we experience from day to day. Until the Impressionists and their immediate precursors took their easels into the open air, artists were generally confined to the studio. (Even a portrait with an outdoor setting would actually be painted in the studio.) Inside the studio the painter would control the amount and direction of the light coming in, using it to simplify and emphasize those aspects of the subject he thought significant. This is very evident in the portraits painted by the Old Masters, where the light seems to fall only on the face and enhances the form. The painter would also try to ensure that the light falling on his subject did not vary. This is why, traditionally, studios face north: light coming from the north generally remains constant throughout the day, whereas light coming from other directions gets warmer as the day progresses.

The bright daylight sought by the Impressionists tends to flatten the subject, making it more difficult to see the simple volumes. And, of course, it is infinitely variable.

Since the Impressionists taught us to regard light and colour as inseparable, we have been inclined to overlook the role of light as an illuminating agent. Consequently, modern paintings tend to be composed of areas of colour rather than areas of light and shade. In modern portraiture, structure is most often sought through the analysis of colour, not through the interplay of light and dark masses. This tendency is reinforced by the images of modern life, in which colour plays a more expressive role than light. The even, strong light that shines on television newsreaders, say, produces a detailed, colourful but rather flat image. On the other hand, most photographs, especially amateur snapshots, are terribly complicated, because the light is coming from many different directions.

The average amateur painter is not going to be able to create the ideal lighting conditions of a traditional artist's studio; nor, perhaps, would he want to. He can, though, learn an important lesson from the Old Masters, and when lighting a subject strive for simplicity. A model should always be posed so that the light is falling as simply as possible. And look for that light against dark effect that gives such a strong, convincing image.

Experiment, moving around a table lamp or even a candle, to see how light affects what you are going to paint. Experiment, too, with different backgrounds – you can learn a lot by just placing pieces of paper or card in various tones and patterns behind your subject.

Another useful exercise is to practise drawing a head, ignoring all the detail and reducing it to simple masses of light and dark. Confine yourself to three tones – dark, light and one middle tone – and try to get the feeling that one side of the head is lit and the other is in shadow.

TONE AND COLOUR

In any painting the relationship between tone and colour is critical.

Tone

The question of tone is a very important one in painting. Most of the shortcomings to be found in amateur painting can be traced to difficulties with tone. Simply, tone is that quality which is measured in degrees on a scale from white to black. The tone of a particular object depends upon two things: its local colour and the amount of light that is falling on it. If things were not coloured, but simply several shades of grey, painting, while being very much less interesting, would be quite a lot easier. The texture of an object plays a part as well: some objects, of course, are matt, others velvety, others shiny, and so on. A dark grey shiny object will reflect more light than the same dark grey in a duller material. I can still remember, many years ago, a tutor pointing out to me that while the lino on the life-room floor was certainly dark brown, consequently much darker than the model, the position from which I was looking at it caused its shiny surface to reflect more than half the light it was receiving. A camera would not have had my knowledge that it was dark lino, so it would have had no problem in recording the tone as it was.

Add colour to texture and the problems are multiplied. Consider the fact that a purple object (purple being a dark colour) in a lot of light can appear lighter than a yellow object (yellow being a light colour) in a lot less light. If you look at a black and white photograph you will see how the registration of light and shade is complicated by the tones of the colours that the photographic process has turned to monochrome.

It is an interesting and useful exercise to look at a scene in front of you (any scene that is not overly complicated), and arrange the tones in ascending or descending order of brightness, assigning the number 0 to white and 10 to black. You can do the same thing with a photograph or a reproduction of a painting.

When you are painting, it often helps initially to separate tone and colour. Look at the sitter and whatever else you are including in the picture and decide which are the lightest and the darkest areas, irrespective of colour. Then, in your mind, arrange the other tones on a scale between. It can also be a good idea to do a tonal drawing or make a monochrome study from time to time. In the past students were required to render certain subjects, particularly antique statuary, in monochrome, almost as though what they were painting was itself without colour, in order to clarify their understanding of the form and structure.

A feeling for tone is especially valuable for the portrait painter, as painting flesh requires a particularly sensitive awareness of small changes of tone. It is a common fault to pitch the tone of flesh too high, so that it looks chalky. Flesh is light, of course, but relatively so (should your model be wearing a white shirt, this will be abundantly clear; if the model is wearing no white, simply hold a piece of white paper against the face – you will see how much darker the flesh is). Again, the tonal gradations found in flesh are very subtle, and in the middle range very close together. The differences in tone between the light and the dark in folds of flesh are on a minute scale compared with different tones in, say, the hair. There is a temptation when you see a fold of flesh to make it too dark, which can destroy the whole tonal balance of a portrait.

Colour

There are many rules of thumb concerning colour and many precise and scientific formulations about the nature of colour and the relationship between the colours themselves. Theories of colour are not an essential part of the artist's repertory of knowledge; a lot of perfectly good, indeed marvellous, pictures have been painted without their help, and too rigid an application of the rules can easily result in a picture which is simply a demonstration of a theory. However, the basic rules are useful, not as something to be consciously applied while actually painting, but as background, guiding information.

Practically everyone knows that a prism divides light up into its constituent hues, and has observed this occurring in the rainbow. The artist also needs to be aware of the relationships between the violet, indigo, blue, green, yellow, orange and red of the spectrum, and to bear in mind the difference between light on the one hand and paint on the other. For example, the colours of the spectrum arranged like segments on a circle will produce white when the circle is revolved at high speed. If you mix those same hues in paint you will produce mud.

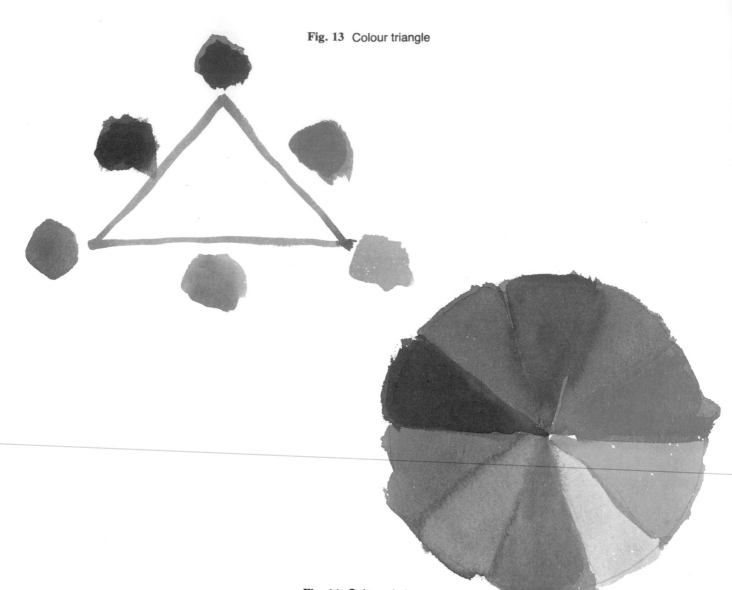

Fig. 13 Colour triangle

Fig. 14 Colour circle

The simplest way of expressing the relationships between the colours and their action on each other is by means of a triangle (**fig. 13**). Make the points of the triangle represent the three primary colours, red, yellow and blue, and the sides of the triangle a mixture of the two primaries at their respective ends. Thus, between red and blue is violet, between blue and yellow is green and between yellow and red is orange. Another, more subtle method of representing these relationships is as a circle (**fig. 14**). Imagine a clock face with red at one o'clock, yellow at five and blue at nine. If you mix red at one o'clock and yellow at five, you will produce orange midway at three o'clock, and so on. The circle gives us a fuller range of hues than the triangle, and on a continuous scale: for example, at two o'clock you have a red-orange and at four, a yellow-orange.

The practical use of this arrangement of colours for the painter lies in the manner in which they act on

each other. In both the triangular and the circular form colours opposite one another are called complementary: so, red is the complementary of green, blue the complementary of orange, yellow the complementary of violet, and so on. In theory an equal mixture of complementaries gives white; in fact it gives a variety of coloured greys. But the practical point about the behaviour of complementaries is that they provide the maximum colour contrast. The red of a poppy against a background of grass is reinforced by the green of the grass. The eye is fatigued by concentrations of a particular colour: its ability to perceive that hue lessens, because the hue's complementary tends to become superimposed, and this blunts the original sensation. Test this yourself by looking at a patch of red or a red object for a minute or so, then look away at white paper. You will see on the paper a pale image of the complementary, in this case green.

20

The opposite of contrast in this context is colour harmony. Harmony is produced by selecting a group of colours from the same segment of the circle: for example, nine o'clock to twelve would be one harmony and one o'clock to four would be another.

Perhaps the most satisfactory method of using colour in a composition is to base it on one colour with its surrounding harmonies, offset with small accents of a complementary or near-complementary (see **fig. 15**).

Another general principle is that all colour can be thought of as either warm or cool, though to convert the thought into precise practice can sometimes be difficult: with green, for example, which has a very wide range. In landscape painting distant hills are generally represented as blue – an instance of the rule that warm colours advance and cold colours retire. (Turner utilized this fact by painting many of his watercolours on blue paper – a built-in distance, so to speak.)

Painting must not be thought of as akin to printing, where the primary colours are mixed by printing one over another, with the addition of black to produce the darks. Indeed, it might be a good idea from time to time to exclude black as a darkening agent from your palette – a phthalo blue or Burnt Umber will produce a tone dark enough for most purposes. The black in the tube is not the same experience as, say, a black hat, or a black motor car, or the coat of a black cat, and black horses are another thing altogether. Your model may have what is called black hair, but there is a great difference between the black of hair and the black of paint.

Certainly you should banish the thought of black in connection with shadows. The colour of a shadow is *not* the local colour of the object plus black – try

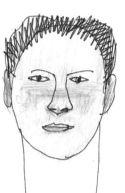

Fig. 16
Colour in the head

mixing black with yellow to produce a shadow on a lemon, say: the result is a dirty green. While all colour must be carefully observed, the colour in shadows is often crucial. However dark the shadow, there will be some hint of warmth or coolness.

As a portrait painter, you should also forget that you can buy paint labelled 'flesh colour'. Try not to think in such categories. No one is uniformly 'flesh-coloured'. In occidental faces, while some are pale and others reddish or swarthy, there is a general allocation of colour areas that is fairly constant. **Fig. 16** is a schematic representation of areas of colour in the head. You will see that the warm colours are mostly in the centre of the face – as in rosy cheeks – but sometimes across the nose as well; accents of stronger red are often found in the ears, or where the nostrils meet the cheek. The forehead is cooler than the cheeks, sometimes markedly so, except across the eyebrows. The neck is usually tinted towards a pale ochre. On men the area where the beard grows is cool, often a quite positive grey-blue.

Another point – don't be fooled by words. The 'whites' of the eyes, for instance, are seldom white. It is the painter's business to *see* what things actually look like.

And the more you concentrate your gaze on anything the more you will tend to see. But there is yet another danger here. It becomes fatally easy to overdo the changes of colour you perceive in the face you are painting. If such complications occur, look away from the model for a few moments and then look back; you should now be able to see more clearly and simply.

In painting everything is relative. You put one colour down, then a second against it, and the two modify each other. Degas once said that the art of painting was to surround, say, a patch of Venetian Red with other colours, and make it appear vermilion.

In the end, colour in use, whether in a painting or in interior decorations, will be a matter of individual taste. It is impossible to argue the fact that red and green produce the effects they do; how such effects are used in a picture is a matter of infinite argument.

Fig. 15 The colour in this pattern of rectangles is based on the yellow, orange, red part of the spectrum, with the addition of a little burnt umber and crimson. The green accents are in fact touches of blue, which on the yellow appear as green.

Fig. 17 *Lester Young* 1987 oil on board 30 × 25 cm/12 × 10 in

Lester Young

In my picture of the musician Lester Young (**fig. 17**) it is the light on the face against the dark background that gives the basic form. The head of the subject stands out clearly against the bold, simple shapes of the background colours. Red in the background really seemed to suggest itself: Young's playing is warm and melodious and passionate, and almost without my thinking about it the picture became warm and darkish in tone. When I had put down the red some coolness seemed necessary to counteract it, so I added the blue. The shadows and darker patches in the face are also slightly bluish, picking up the background colour. In choosing these particular colours, I think I must also have had in the back of my mind an image of the colours, lighting and general atmosphere of a jazz club.

COMPOSITION

The basic approach to painting a portrait is the same no matter what medium you are using. Obviously, different mediums tend to result in different sorts of images, but the underlying concerns will be the same. In the following pages I will outline these concerns as they arise in the actual business of painting. I will include hints and observations that are the products of my experience – another artist may well give you a different list.

All painting operates through drawing, colour and tone. Different periods have favoured different proportions of these ingredients, just as different individuals will, as well as different genres of painting. Whatever the ratio, however, while you are actually painting, they are in the air at the same time, like balls or Indian clubs.

From my experience, I would say that the central plank of portraiture is drawing: not drawing for its own sake, but drawing to establish measurement, angles, lengths, changes of direction.

Likenesses result from drawing, that is, the process of drawing which takes place continuously in a painting. The foundation of this kind of drawing is looking hard at the subject. Indeed, the importance of just looking cannot be overemphasized. For example, if you spend an hour painting something, at least fifteen minutes of that hour should be taken up with simply looking, rather than doing. The looking will familiarize you with the subject's over-all characteristics and may cause you to modify the pose and lighting.

Before you start your painting, give some thought to how the model is to sit, bearing in mind that he or she has to be comfortable, and that you need a pose that makes a good shape on the canvas. (If you are painting over several sittings, and if circumstances allow, mark the exact position of the model's chair, and that of the feet.)

Once the pose is decided, the next step is to assess the model's basic proportions. The process of measuring, checking measurements, and taking measurements of increasingly small details, should continue all through the painting.

The traditional way of measuring is to hold your brush up at arm's length and check off distances against the brush-end. Before you start your painting, note the size of the head, and how many times it goes into the amount of body you have showing. (Usually, the head will go into the full-length adult figure about seven and a half times.) Later, you

Fig. 18 *The Artist's Wife* 1982 pencil drawing

will need to check the smaller measurements. For example, measure the width of the shoulder in relation to the length of the head, the height of the forehead in relation to the length of the nose, and so on. Plumb a line through the model from some prominent feature, say the edge of a nostril or the corner of an eye. (Until you have the experience to assess this by eye, use a plumb line. It is very easy to make one – just tie any small weight, such as a bunch of keys, on to a length of black thread.) Note what other features are cut by the line, and rule a corresponding line on the canvas. Keep checking this line throughout the painting, and every now and again plumb other features in the same way.

As well as vertical checks, use your brush handle as a ruler to measure horizontal angles, for example, the angle through the eyes, or through the shoulders. These things are not approximate, neither are they a matter of guesswork.

At the outset, work out which parts of the model are nearest to you, and try to see the head, as it were, in perspective. Decide where on your canvas (or board, or paper, or whatever), the head is to be, and then where the rest of the body will be in relation to it. Have you got room for the hands, or will the edges of the canvas disastrously chop them off at the wrists? Indicate the basic proportions with charcoal.

If you feel quite confident of your composition you can work directly on to the canvas. But you may find that it helps to make a small rough plan in a notebook, or on a bit of paper, first. Draw a rectangle in proportion to the canvas and sketch your plan inside it. Enlarging a drawing on to a canvas is quite a straightforward affair. Just place the rectangle that frames your sketch on the bottom left-hand corner of your canvas. Draw a diagonal through the rectangle and continue it till you reach the enlargement you want: any pair of vertical and horizontal lines that meet at the diagonal will produce a rectangle in proportion to the original, as shown in **fig. 19a**.

Draw a second diagonal across the canvas, to bisect the first, then draw a vertical and a horizontal line across the centre. The first rectangle is now divided into four smaller rectangles. Draw diagonal lines from corner to corner across each of these. Continue in this way (**fig. 19b**) till the grid is as fine as you require. Number the rectangles if you need to. Indicate on the canvas what occurs in the corresponding rectangle in your plan (**fig. 19c**).

Now take a large brush and block in the main colour areas very broadly, thinking about the look of the canvas as a whole and seeing the colours as shapes. At this stage do not linger on features, do not think about expressions, avoid speculations about the model's nature and psychology. Simply concentrate on the large shapes and the underlying

structure and how they fit together. Sargent said that features bore the same relation to the head as spots do on the skin of an apple. He was exaggerating, of course, but on the side of truth. It is a useful notion to bear in mind.

When you have the basic shapes you can start to tighten up the drawing, but still avoiding details. At this stage you should be refining the shapes, in rather the way you would if you were making a model. If you are making a model you can't start with the features, because you have nothing to put the features on: you have to start with the big shapes. And it is the sense of the big shape that you should carry through your portrait. Amateur painters often get arrested by detail, thinking, perhaps, that that is where the essence of character lies.

When you do start to work on the head in a bit more detail, do not lose sight of the structure and over-all shape of the face. Starting with the eye nearer to you, gradually increase the definition of the features. Watch the tones very carefully at this stage. For example, it is a common fault in inexperienced painters to get the tones under the eyebrows or under the nostrils far too dark. Leave the mouth,

Fig. 19 Enlarging a drawing

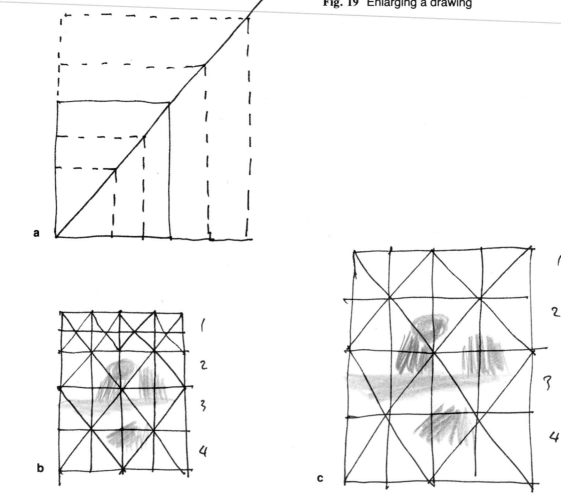

Fig. 20 *The Artist's Wife* 1986 pastel study for a portrait

which is the most mobile feature, till the very end. Expression evolves, and you don't want to fix it too early. One of the worst, most inhibiting things that can happen is to get a satisfactory expression almost by accident and consequently be forced to paint the portrait round it.

If you are sitting to paint, get up every so often and look at the painting from a different viewpoint and from further away. The eye gets used to what it is seeing and the important discrepancies between the picture and the model get lost. Looking from a fresh position will help you to see the picture anew. So, incidentally, will looking at it in a mirror. If you can arrange it so that the image of your painting and that of the model are side by side and the same size in the mirror, so much the better.

Louise

The fact that painting is a business of trial and error is rather painfully illustrated by the progress of this painting – intended, initially, as a straightforward demonstration of technique.

First stage I decided where on the canvas the head was to be, indicated it with a few charcoal lines and very roughly marked in the positions of the arms and hands in relation to it. I made one or two quick

RIGHT **Fig. 21** First stage

25

measurements of proportion, checking the distance from the top of the head to the chin and comparing that with the distance between the chin and the forearm. Then I reinforced the charcoal marks (**fig. 21**).

Second stage I then laid in the basic shapes and colours. I put down flesh colour in a flat area to indicate the face and neck, making no attempt at modelling. Against this I set the shape of the hair, the flat shape of the body, the chair, until the canvas was covered. Then I returned to the head and indicated very broadly the position of the eyes, the bottom of the nose, the lips and the bottom of the chin (**fig. 22**).

By this time I was fairly uneasy about the colours. I seldom base colour schemes on contrast, preferring to work with related main colours, accented here and there with contrasts. In this case I had departed from my usual procedure. I had not asked Louise to wear a viridian sweatshirt, she just happened to be wearing it, but I am always attracted by that particular blue-green, and I was happy to use it. The problems had begun when, without thinking hard enough about it, I sat her down in the pink chair in my studio. The strong

contrast between the pink and the green was now definitely beginning to look like a mistake. However, it is very difficult to abandon a painting on which you have expended some labour. As so often, I went on, in the hope that the problem would right itself.

Third stage Starting to measure more precisely now, I marked the planes of the face, the angles of the nose. I noted exactly where the corner of the eye came against the inside of the bridge of the nose. From that point I drew a vertical line in charcoal right through the figure, from the top of the head to the bottom of the canvas. I held my brush up to correspond to the line and checked where it intersected other significant bits of the painting, such as the arm, the neck, and so on. Then I checked the features (for example, the length of the nose) against this line. When I felt that the head was beginning to take shape, I checked the proportions of the other parts of the picture against it. I drew a line to indicate corrections, then painted up to the line (**fig. 23**).

ABOVE LEFT **Fig. 22** Second stage
ABOVE RIGHT **Fig. 23** Third stage

26

Completed portrait When I got to this point, I was forced to acknowledge that the picture needed drastic rethinking. Far from improving matters, I had been reinforcing a failure. This again is a common experience. When a picture goes wrong in one area it can very quickly go wrong in a lot of others – like panic spreading. Difficulties with composition soon become difficulties of drawing, and the painting as a portrait starts to disintegrate before you eyes. Which is what is happening here, in **fig. 24**. My initial diagnosis of the problem concentrated, wrongly as it turned out, on the colours. I replaced the pink chair with one upholstered in greyish-green, so the colour scheme became a sort of harmony of greens and greys, with the flesh providing the warm tones. However, once I had started to work with colours I actually liked, it became increasingly apparent that the figure did not fit well in the rectangle of the canvas. I also became aware that the light on the figure as a whole, and particularly on the face, was too flat. I finally decided to start from the beginning again, using a canvas of the same size as the one I had used for my first attempt, but turning it on its side, to give landscape proportions. I left the pose more or less the same, but turned the chair away from the light a little, to produce some definite modelling on the figure. I find this second version (**fig. 25**) much more satisfactory than the first.

LEFT **Fig. 24** *Louise* 1988 oil on canvas 76 × 56 cm/30 × 22 in
BELOW **Fig. 25** *Louise* 1988 oil on canvas 56 × 76 cm/22 × 30 in

Fig. 26 First stage

Fig. 27
Second stage

Michael Leonard

Before I paint a portrait I often do exploratory drawings, to test whether the pose is going to work and sometimes as a way of accustoming myself to the model's features and expressions. As in this case, when I come to the portrait itself I often use a completely different pose.

When I start a drawing I like to keep it as fluid and as lively as I can. The degree of finish on drawings such as this seems to be quite arbitrary. I am doing the drawing for information, not for its own sake, so what it looks like is less important than what I learn from it.

First stage The most important thing at this stage is to get to know the subject in terms of basic shapes and proportions. Using a 2B pencil and concentrating entirely on proportion, structure and mass, I marked in the large shapes (**fig. 26**).

Second stage I started to explore the shapes inside the face, for example around the nostrils, using my pencil to produce tone and taking out the highlights with a putty rubber (**fig. 27**). A reasonably heavy paper, such as the 290 gsm (140 lb) HP paper used here, will take quite a lot of rubbing.

When you are painting in oils, if you make an error you can paint it out with solid colour; you can't do this with watercolour. So a watercolour portrait requires more caution than a portrait in oils. The difficulty is that at the same time it demands more confidence and panache, because nothing will kill a watercolour more quickly than an excessively tentative approach. Most people, including myself, are tempted to use washes that are too pale, fearing to apply a wash that is too dark for flesh, and also hoping that, if necessary, it will be possible to put on darker washes later. In fact the tone of flesh is usually darker than you think. And if you are going to err, it is better to put on a wash that is too dark than one that is too light. You can sponge off a dark wash while it is still damp, but if you apply too many washes, in series, the picture will lose all spontaneity, and the surface will look tired.

But it will help you to avoid difficulties in determining tone if you establish as early as possible which is the lightest or the darkest area you are going to paint.

Third stage First I marked in the general shape, just marking rough indications in pencil. I did not rub out these pencil lines – rubbing roughs up the paper, and then the wash will go on badly. Most pencil lines disappear under a wash, even a pale wash. The next step is to look for the darkest or the lightest area, to establish a key for the tones. The darkest areas here were clearly Michael's hair and the dark navy jacket he was wearing (**fig. 28**).

28

Fig. 28 Third stage

Fig. 29 Fourth stage

Fourth stage At this stage I began working with more precision, adding colour and shape at the same time. It is important to work all over the picture, not just on the head – remember, all the tones are relative.

Fig. 30 *Michael Leonard* 1986
watercolour 36 × 27 cm/14 × 10½ in

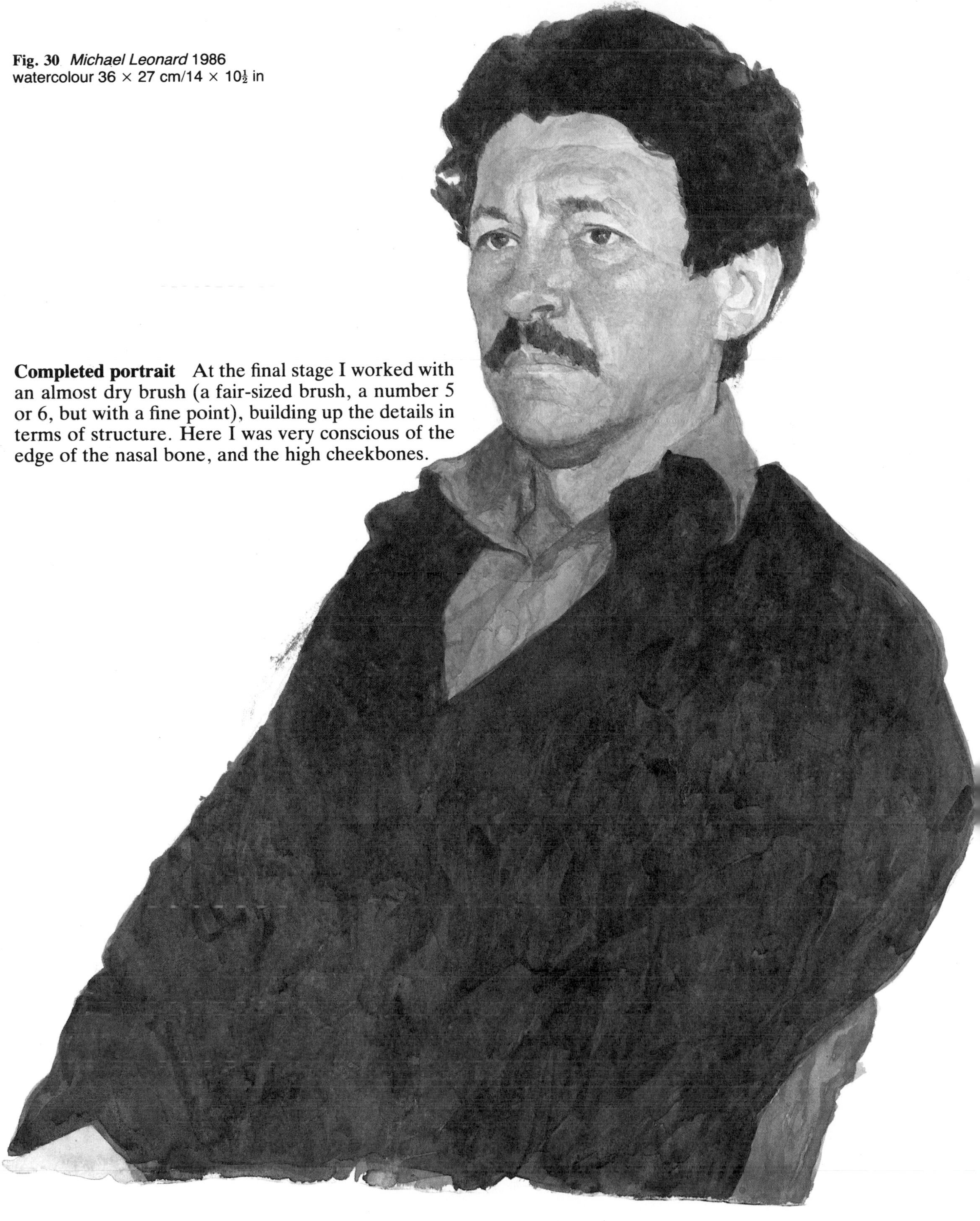

Completed portrait   At the final stage I worked with
an almost dry brush (a fair-sized brush, a number 5
or 6, but with a fine point), building up the details in
terms of structure. Here I was very conscious of the
edge of the nasal bone, and the high cheekbones.

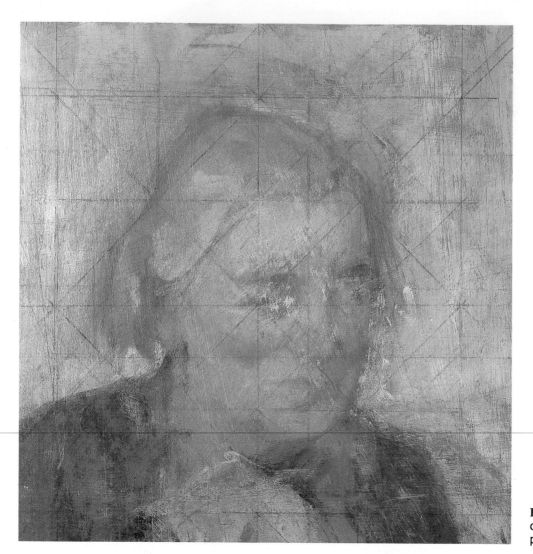

Fig. 31 *The Artist's Mother* 1986 oil on wooden panel, an unfinished portrait 36 × 36 cm/14 × 14 in

Fig. 32 *The Artist's Mother* 1986 oil on wooden panel 25 × 30 cm/10 × 12 in

The Artist's Mother

Fig. 33 *The Artist's Mother* 1986 pastel 28 × 38 cm/11 × 15 in

Fig. 31 shows a first attempt at a portrait of my mother. I abandoned it because I wanted the head to fill more of the board. The first panel I chose was too large in itself, so if I had done the portrait in the proportions I wanted the head would have been too big. Also, at that time I didn't like the way the painting was going. Now I feel that, unfinished as it is, it has a kind of simplicity which perhaps the finished oil lacks. This second oil (**fig. 32**) is a reasonably accurate likeness, I suppose, but personally I find it a bit dull.

The pastel shown in **fig. 33** was done half-way through the painting of the second oil. I was getting too niggling and obsessed with details, and needed a fresh perspective. The change of medium (pastel is of its nature a broader medium than oil) and use of a different pose made it much easier to see the essential character and nature of the face. Also, the fact that the side of the face is lit and the features are in shadow gives a more immediate sense of solidity.

Prokofiev studies

And when is a portrait completed? It is hard to know, sometimes. Completeness is an intangible quality, very difficult to describe. I would make a distinction here between completeness and finish. You can have a very detailed, very 'finished' painting which yet seems incomplete because the composition is not satisfying. On the other hand, you can have a very sketchy work which is, somehow, complete. If a portrait is properly composed you can stop it, as it were, at a particular level, when all the parts are right in relation to each other.

I painted these studies (**figs. 34** and **35**) of Prokofiev (from photographs) after listening to his *Visions fugitives*. I love Prokofiev's music, and I wanted to do a picture which in some way reflected my admiration. When I started I didn't know quite what I was going to do, except that I didn't want to do a straight academic portrait. I stopped both these studies at a fairly early stage: it seemed to me that they had a certain completeness at that point. I started other, more conventional, portraits, but abandoned them.

ABOVE **Fig. 34** *Prokofiev* 1978 watercolour 30 × 30 cm/ 12 × 12 in
RIGHT **Fig. 35** *Prokofiev* 1978 watercolour 21 × 33 cm/ 8½ × 13 in.

VARIOUS MEDIUMS

Choice of medium is by no means always a rational matter. For instance, I did not use watercolour for years, for no better reason than that I could not imagine myself using it. Perhaps this was simply because the physical substance of oil paint has always appealed to me so much.

I would not recommend any student of painting to switch methodically from medium to medium just for the sake of experience. It is preferable to get some kind of confidence with one medium and then move into other areas as the mood takes you. Your choice of medium can depend, of course, on the kind of subject that attracts you: for example, if you want to paint a landscape, watercolour could well be your first choice as a medium. A portrait, on the other hand, usually suggests oil or acrylic – anyway, a 'solid' medium where adjustments can be made throughout the course of painting.

A change of medium forces a change of tactics, or it ought to. You cannot produce the same kind of image in, for example, pastel as you can in watercolour. You are in a sense in partnership with the medium – it affects what you do, even how you see, as you attempt to give an image shape and coherence.

The six paintings in **figs. 36–41** are all versions of the same portrait, each done in a different medium. They illustrate fairly clearly the characteristics of the various mediums, as well as how different mediums seem to lead to different interpretations of the subject. This latter point underlines the principle that there is no such thing as one 'right' likeness.

For example, with a portrait in line, the size of the image is going to be very much related to the thickness of the line: if you are using an instrument that produces a fine line, the image cannot be very large, or the line would become meaningless. For this reason, the image in a pen or pencil drawing tends to be small. A brush, on the other hand, produces a big, bold line: consequently, the image in a brush drawing will be bold. Oil paint allows a great variety of treatments, from sketchy to highly finished, whereas, because it permits only limited correction, watercolour tends to invite spontaneity and informality. With oils or watercolours colours are mixed

Fig. 36 Pencil

Fig. 37 Pen and ink

Fig. 38 Brush drawing

Fig. 40 Pastel

Fig. 39 Watercolour

Fig. 41 Oil

on the palette; but with pastels, the colours are mixed on the paper itself, one colour being superimposed over another. And often, as here, using pastels leads to richer, sometimes brighter, colour.

In short, the medium the painter uses will require him to select different aspects of his subject for emphasis, and to minimize or exclude others.

ABOVE **Fig. 42** *David Skeggs* 1986 oil on wooden panel 30 × 25 cm/12 × 10 in
ABOVE RIGHT **Fig. 43** *David Skeggs* 1982 pencil study for portrait
RIGHT **Fig. 44** *David Skeggs* 1982 oil on paper 30 × 36 cm/12 × 14 in

ABOVE LEFT **Fig. 45** *David Skeggs* 1985 watercolour study for portrait
ABOVE **Fig. 46** *David Skeggs* 1986 pastel 55 × 37 cm/ 21½ × 14½ in
LEFT **Fig. 47** *David Skeggs* 1986 pastel 35 × 50 cm/ 13¾ × 20 in

THE USE OF PHOTOGRAPHY

Photography, after terrifying painters at its invention in the middle of the last century, has now been more or less accommodated by them, and may certainly influence what they produce. In one sense the whole development of modern art can be seen as a consequence of the camera's usurping the painter's principal, traditional role as a reporter of what things look like, allowing him to wander along more irrational and more decorative paths.

More directly, many painters have used photographs as a basis for paintings. The exponents of Pop Art, of course, are famous for using photographs, often taken from newspapers and magazines. Pop Art painters frequently emphasize the 'photographic' qualities of the photograph – distortions, for example, created by accidents of light and movement or the peculiarities of the lens. Other artists, among them the painters known as Photo-Realists, simply use the photograph as a thing in itself and render it, edge to edge, on a large scale. Most painters, some aware, some unaware of the camera's idiosyncrasies, simply use photographs as a short cut, or for convenience: nature at one remove, as it were. But in the last analysis it is not why but how photography is used that counts. The finished painting is proof of the efficacy, or otherwise, of the method.

More portraits are painted with the aid of photographs than you would imagine, and have been for far longer than is generally reckoned. For example, there is clear evidence that some of the Impressionists, and before them Ingres and Delacroix, used photographs. Some people have raised moral objections to such procedures, implying that only in the presence of the model can any kind of genuine response be sparked. It is certainly true that it is always better to have a model in front of you: somehow the presence of a living model allows you the freedom to use your imagination, while a photograph tends to tie you to its image. But it is often simply impossible to have your sitter always present. Certainly the important men painted by the Old Masters did not sit around in artists' studios for months, or days. Holbein's portraits, for example, were almost always painted from drawings, done in a relatively short time from the sitter. Indeed, it is said that Holbein would draw with paint on a glass placed between himself and the sitter, with a fixed eye-piece to look through to stop the image appearing to jog about, and take a 'print' from the glass to form the basis of his composition. Vermeer used a *camera obscura* – a device which projected an inverted image of the subject on to a ground glass screen from which the salient features could be traced off.

To professional artists, including portrait painters, the camera offers convenience and speed, both great advantages; but such advantages have to be paid for. The first point to be borne in mind, when using a photograph as the basis for a painting, is that a photograph is already a pictorial statement: it has qualities of its own. Sometimes these will be accidental, sometimes the fruits of conscious deliberation. Either way, all photographs are at one remove from reality: they constitute the representation of three dimensions on a flat surface, as does painting itself. Photography is often invoked as a standard by which the objectivity of a representation can be judged – 'It's just like a photograph', people say, intending to praise a painting's fidelity to nature. Most photographs, however, present a very schematic and distorted way of dealing with reality.

Among the factors that influence the character of photographs are, first of all, the subject, then the lens, the speed of the film, the lighting conditions, the method of processing, the experience of the photographer, and the relations between all these. For example, if you take a photograph of a landscape with a range of low hills, say two miles distant, using a camera fitted with a standard lens, it will appear strikingly different from your perception of the landscape itself. The hills will dwindle to an insignificant strip apparently many miles away.

With a closer subject, as in a portrait, equivalent distortions can occur. The features nearest to the lens, usually the nose, become enlarged out of all proportion to the rest of the face – not a reliable basis for painting a likeness.

Another characteristic of photography that can be a disadvantage in a source of reference is its way with tones. Tones similar in degree become amalgamated: at the top end of the scale this means that light areas tend to bleed into an undifferentiated patch containing little or no information. The loss in these situations of the actual highlights is serious, for they indicate exactly where a form changes direction, and the forehead, say, or the nose, is reduced to a smear of off-white. At the opposite end of the scale the same thing occurs. Objects in shadow and dark objects, in shadow or not, lose definition and melt together in large, impenetrable areas of dark. As a further consequence of all this, transitions from light

Fig. 48 Studies for a portrait of Ezra Pound 1984 brush drawing

to dark become abrupt and unsubtle compared with the nuances available from nature. Half-tones are very important to the painter, as are the characteristics of forms in shadows, and he is not well served by the camera here.

Of course, there have been times when painters have been able actually to use the kind of simplification forced on them by the use of photography. Manet, in his revolt against the academic procedures of his day, used such effects with great aplomb. Walter Sickert was another painter who used the distortions inherent in photography in his paintings. (It was Sickert, however, who recommended that only those artists who can do without them should use photographs.)

Again, we must remember that the camera, being a mechanical device, has no judgement. It is as though we all possess some kind of filing system modified by experience, in which is contained a sort of master set of acceptable likenesses of people whose faces we know; and that we unconsciously reject those moments when some involuntary gesture, say sneezing, deforms the familiar features. The camera has no such value system, and is able, into the bargain, to record at fractions of a second. Consequently, it can produce sadly or comically bad likenesses of people. It is perfectly possible for an experienced photographer to expose many rolls of film in a portrait session and get only one or two reasonable pictures.

Flash photography produces its own special version of reality. In a photograph taken with the aid of a flash there will be an even, flattish light on the subject, with small, dark shadows at the edges of forms, strong highlights in the middle of a dark iris, and a black background, hardly natural and very characteristic of its kind.

The special usefulness of colour photography is that objects tend to be defined by their local colour, accurate or not, thus giving us more information. But it must be remembered that the colour on offer is only one of a number of possible versions. Had the sun come out, or gone in, when the shutter clicked, had the processor been different, had you pointed the camera up or down slightly, the colour would have turned out differently.

Any artist using photography in his work ought, at the very least, to be aware of its basic characteristics. Better still, he should take the photographs himself rather than depend on those of others. A 'found' photograph does not provide you with much information outside itself; you do not know how accurate an interpretation it is (unless, of course, you have a separate knowledge of the subject). If you take your own photographs your awareness of the circumstances pertaining to but not included in the photograph will be greater. Also, you can try to avoid some of the more obvious pitfalls at the outset.

Whether you are taking or choosing a photograph to be used as the basis for a portrait, the requirements are the same. The lighting should be simple and definite, not diffused, nor coming from different directions with useless reflected lights. Remember, the object is to make the shape of the head and the relationship of the features clear and immediate and straightforward in design. Ensure, by asking yourself questions and making thumbnail sketches, that the photograph you intend to use is, in fact, usable. Often, what appears at the outset to be adequate turns out, after some hours of work, to be much less than satisfactory.

If you are choosing photographs of, say, the great and famous from magazines, avoid on principle pictures by star photographers. The qualities of a painting based on such a photograph are likely to come from the photographer rather than from you.

At the other end of the scale, family snaps can be an equally dangerous source of information. Be wary of arbitrary light, strangely caught expressions, cut-off feet, eyes squinting into the sun, and similar effects! But, having said that, even quite poor photographs can be useful if they are carefully scrutinized and considered before painting begins. Many things happen by accident in photography which can be a useful source of inspiration for the artist.

To sum up: do not be tricked into thinking that photographs are generally 'correct' renditions of the world. Be aware of the differences between your own natural vision and the camera's version, and do not 'copy' a photograph tone for tone, but use it for information. Sense the underlying structure, and interpret what the gradations of tone mean in terms of real flesh and bone.

Katie and her Godmother

I took the photograph of my daughter Katie with her godmother (**fig. 49**) at her christening. I came across it several years later, at a time when I was interested in the idea of painting a portrait of a baby, and used it as the basis for the portrait (**fig. 50**).

I tried to use the photograph, rather than copy it. You can see how I edited out the figure in the background, and reduced the whole area to concentrate on the relationship between the two heads. I interpreted the pattern on the dress in a pictorial rather than a literal way, using the actual print as an excuse to invent a decorative pattern that works in terms of the painting.

Fig. 49 A photograph of my daughter Katie with her godmother, at her christening, 1975

Fig. 50 *Katie and her Godmother* 1980 oil on wooden panel 30 × 36 cm/12 × 14 in

42

Olivier Messiaen

The immediate inspiration for this portrait (**fig. 51**) was a badly reproduced black and white photograph in a magazine. For some time I had at the back of my mind the idea of painting a picture of the composer, as a gift for a friend who shares my passion for the music of Messiaen. But I didn't actually start to paint until I happened to see the photograph, and was fascinated by the pattern of abstract shapes against the bleached-out background.

Fig. 51 *Olivier Messiaen* 1969 watercolour
48 × 33 cm/19 × 13 in

WHAT CAN GO WRONG ?

A painting may go wrong because of the subject, or the composition, or the drawing, or the colour, or the tone values, singly or in any combination. As well as these technical problems there are psychological difficulties which can lead to various blockages and strange notions, which in turn lead to all kinds of odd things happening on the canvas. But these psychological problems are very individual and need to be sorted out individually. I can only deal here with the technical problems that are most likely to occur in the process of painting a portrait.

Errors in painting from nature can result from, on the one hand, cursory observation, or, on the other, inexpert handling of the picture itself, or from a combination of the two. The first can be corrected at the outset by making diligent observation a habit; the second, of course, is corrected by experience itself. Experience, however, can be assisted.

Composition

Very often students pay too little attention to composition in portrait painting. They seem to feel that if the likeness is all right the rest of the painting does not matter. This is not so. Even if there is nothing else in the painting than the head and neck, as in many Old Masters, the positioning of the head in relation to the size and proportions of the canvas is very important. And you can easily get the head in the wrong place. Of course the 'wrong place' is in the end a matter of judgement and taste – what to one person is an interesting or intriguing placement, to another will seem simply perverse. However, what I would advocate for the student is a responsible and moderate approach.

Some examples of unsatisfactory positioning are illustrated in **fig. 52**. In **fig. 52a** the head looks as if it is being compressed by the top edge of the canvas, and the main area of the canvas is without significant incident. Also, the figure is symmetrically arranged on a central vertical axis. In **fig. 52b** symmetry is avoided, which is basically a good idea, but the means of avoidance are too violent. Unless you are very sure of what you are doing, it is wiser not to crop bits off the head. In **fig. 52c** the effect of placing the head at the bottom of the canvas is nearly comical. The positioning of the head is also too symmetrical. And remember that if you wish to use the head alone, the canvas ought not to be too big in relation to the size of the head.

Drawing

In this context I mean not drawing for its own sake, but those aspects of portrait painting that involve drawing in some form or other. Drawing is the skeleton, the framework of a portrait, and generally when something goes wrong with the likeness it is the drawing that is at fault.

Faulty drawing can result from insufficient observation, not looking hard enough at what is being drawn and not looking at the whole while drawing. For example, if you are drawing the nose, do not keep the eyes riveted on that: look at it, assess its shape, colour, and so on, but then look at the head as a whole.

By far the biggest problem students face is the business of relating the features to the head as a whole shape, set upon the neck and shoulders. It is probably human nature to concentrate our attention on the features: when children, for instance, draw a 'portrait' they tend to group eyes, nose and mouth more or less in the natural order, but to show no interest in the shape, proportion or size of the head itself. The human face is such a powerful image that we can assemble it from the scantiest of clues. But, as students of portrait painting, it is precisely this we have to unlearn; to the portrait painter likenesses are not simply the sum of a collection of features.

So, keep relating one part to another. Do not guess at things like the angle of the shoulders or the depth of the forehead; measure them in the old-fashioned way – arm extended, checking the distances off against the brush-end. Measure, too, proportions within the whole figure, as described on page 23. With experience, the basic proportions can be gauged by eye, almost unconsciously, but however adept you get they still need to be checked and corrections made throughout the painting.

Colour and tone

Drawing is a matter of quantity, that is, a lot of it is to do with measuring – an angle is either acute or obtuse, for example. Colour, of course, is not like this: it tends to be a matter of quality; and of personal taste. It is impossible to know whether or not two people looking at a colour are in fact seeing the same colour.

Problems with colour and tone in portraiture run along a few well-worn grooves. (It can be comforting

Fig. 52 Examples of unsatisfactory positioning

a

b

c

45

Fig. 53 *Katie in the Snow* 1986 oil on board 20 × 25 cm/8 × 10 in. I always find figures in snow exciting – both visually and because of the echoes of childhood. Flesh against snow looks very rich. But it was the hat, as much as anything, that made me paint this picture.

to remember that the mess you are in has claimed practically all artists at some point in their careers, however good they might be.) Here I will comment on the most fundamental and debilitating ones. These come in pairs of opposites, simply expressed as too little or too much colour and too high or too low tone.

An anaemic, tentative painting is sometimes simply the reflection of a general want of confidence, but sometimes it is the consequence of indifferent observation. In this second case, more careful observation will help it into life. In the occidental human head, warm and cool tints are contrasted (see **fig. 16**). But if the light parts of a picture get too light, they tend to merge in an unnatural, undifferentiated pinkish-white tint, as if the model's complexion were that of a plastic doll. Dark parts too can easily become uniform and monochrome, especially if too

much black is used: remember that shadows are coloured.

At the opposite end of the scale, too much colour can impair both the design of the painting and the clarity of the actual portrait. The problem is that the more you look the more colour changes you will see in the model. To get this kind of confusion under control, you must institute some comparative scrutiny. That is, you have to compare one passage of colour on the model with another, and put your conclusions into words. For example, you might feel that a particular area of the face is quite warm, with a fair amount of red in it. However, when you compare it with another part, say across the cheeks, it may seem hardly red at all.

Tone and colour are, as we have seen (pages 19–22), closely related; and an error in one can lead to an error in the other. For instance, if the tone of a

Fig. 54 Studies of heads 1986 pen and ink

painting is too high, the colour will be driven out for the sake of achieving light tones. In a portrait, this will inevitably mean that flesh looks unpleasantly chalky. Moreover, you will find that you run out of light, so to speak: a situation that will become apparent when you are faced with a bright highlight or a white shirt.

Spend some time in deciding just what tone the flesh is – it is usually darker than you at first imagine. And do not think of light as white pigment.

Similarly, too dark a picture will obviously drive out colour, as it will tend to invite black as the darkening agent, and local colour plus black is not the way low tones are best achieved.

On the subject of shadows, remember that unless the illumination is concentrated and intense, the shadow side of the face will be much lighter than the shadow side of a business suit, for instance.

Mouths

Finally, a lot can go wrong with the mouth. Indeed, Sargent described a portrait as a likeness in which something is wrong with the mouth. It goes wrong simply because the mouth is the most mobile part of the face. In the faces we know, we are aware of a repertory of expressions, and in our notion of that face, our mind's eye portrait of it, the expression tends to be unfocused, an amalgam of all the expressions we can recall. Specific expressions, such as misery or (*pace* Frans Hals) laughter, are to be avoided, because they tend to become boring to look at. Usually, in a good portrait the expression is ambiguous – think of the *Mona Lisa*! Forget all notions of characterization or psychology, allow the mouth to evolve, and try to create a likeness without drawing too much attention to it.

47

EXTENDING THE TRADITIONAL PORTRAIT

A portrait should be more than a good likeness. It is possible to have a good likeness in a bad picture, just as it is possible to have a good picture which is an indifferent likeness. The problem of portrait painting is to incorporate a good likeness into a good picture.

It is said that painting consists of two quite separate elements, the 'what' and the 'how' – the 'what' being the subject and the 'how' the design and execution. It is also said that artists are more interested in the 'how' and laymen more interested in the 'what'. Like all generalizations, this statement is over-simplified; but it does contain an important point, which applies in a rather special way to portraits. I, for example, have on occasions been so excited by the pictorial qualities of a painting – drawing, composition, the handling of paint, that kind of thing – that it has not

occurred to me to consider the subject consciously at all, beyond perhaps noting that the picture is a landscape, or a figure, or what have you. If I walk into a room containing pictures that I have not seen before, after looking around I would always examine first the painting whose pattern quality, if you like, its abstract character, I found the most immediately

BELOW **Fig. 55** *Hannah and Daisy* 1985 watercolour 28 × 38 cm/11 × 15 in. The picture is intended to be a portrait of the dog as well as of the child – though my attention was first caught by how Hannah looked at a moment when she was sulking, and wearing a cap of mine. I have always liked painting subjects against the light.
OPPOSITE **Fig. 56** *Hannah* 1984 watercolour 38 × 28 cm/15 × 11 in

48

appealing, regardless of whether the painting was a landscape, or a figure, or a still-life. Someone whose prime interest was the subject-matter, however, might say, 'Oh dear, still-life there, another still-life here, and a street scene, no – ah, there's a landscape, and a river too' – and investigate further only those paintings with subjects that appealed to him.

Some subjects, particularly landscape, are full of associations, memories of other times, notions of the past or of unvisited places. This goes far to explain the universal popularity of landscape painting as a genre. Compared with such riches, the portrait as a category comes off rather badly. It does, indeed, partake of what is, in general terms, perhaps the most fascinating subject of all, the human face. But the fact remains that the subject of any particular portrait is likely to be of interest only when the spectator knows the sitter, either personally or by repute. Any interest beyond that must come from the 'how'. And here the genre of portrait painting has been painfully limited. If you think again of the ranks of faces decorating the walls of stately homes, the limitations of the repertory of composition in the traditional portrait will quickly become evident. Throughout the heyday of portrait painting the choice available to portrait painters was confined to three or four poses: head and shoulders; half-length with hands clasped or with one hand delicately supporting the chin; and full-length; all against a dark, un-particularized background. Whichever pose was adopted, the attention was concentrated on the head, frequently to the detriment of the figure as a whole. (Often, bodies were painted from draped dummies, and hands were painted from stand-ins, or generalized to the point of formula.) Of course, the tradition of portrait painting has produced many surpassing works, alongside the more humble, the honest, and the dull. The intrinsic qualities of a portrait by Van Dyck, for instance, or Gainsborough, are obvious almost at a glance: in these portraits the 'how' has become more important than the 'what'. But most people find it difficult to respond to the general run of portraits with anything much more than bored admiration – unless, indeed, they are related to, or have a special interest in, the sitter.

Many portraits painted at the end of the last century hint at an impatience with the traditional layout. Looking, for example, at the marvellous portraits of Degas, you can see him working his way out of an exhausted form. Today the traditional portrait, except in the most distinguished hands, tends to be something of a cliché.

I would like my portraits to work as pictures in their own right, and I often find it easier to achieve this if I move away from the traditional format, and introduce other elements.

Fig. 57 *The Artist's Wife at Sandwich* 1986 watercolour study for a painting. I started to paint this picture simply because I liked the figure walking on wet sand, and I developed it into a portrait (albeit without features) as I worked. It is also a portrait of a landscape, at Pegwell Bay – the subject of a Pre-Raphaelite painting by William Dyce which I have loved as long as I can remember.

Roger Ackling 1985

Figures in a landscape

In portraits I have painted of my two daughters, for example, I have got progressively further away from them, and included more background. This of course means that the figures of the girls themselves become smaller, in some cases very small indeed. Obviously, in such pictures the faces, usually the focal point of a portrait, become less capable of showing detail. Consequently, the body as a whole becomes the subject of the portrait. Since we, in the twentieth century, know how much not only our faces but our whole bodies are governed by our minds, a portrait of a body seems not so very unusual. It is not only the face which is distinctive. You can always recognize someone you know well from a distance, long before it is possible to distinguish the features. Everyone has his or her own way of standing, or sitting. And the masses, the big shapes, of the head, or the neck, for instance, are quite distinctive.

OPPOSITE **Fig. 58** Compositional studies for *Children with Coke* and *The Fence* 1986 pencil and pen and ink
BELOW **Fig. 59** Study for *Children with Coke* 1986 watercolour

Fig. 60 *Children with Coke* 1986 oil on board 25 × 30 cm/10 × 12 in. I like to see how much of a likeness I can get without portraying the features in an obvious way. 'Figures in a landscape' is a traditional theme. The landscape here is that around the village where I live. The actual situation arose while we were out walking: a friend had given the girls cans of Coke, and the red tins looked marvellous against the green of the downs.

LEFT **Fig. 61** *The Fence* 1986 oil on board 30 × 40 cm/
12 × 16 in. Here again the landscape is that around my home.
The two girls are opposites in temperament, and I think some of
the rivalry between them comes across in this picture.
ABOVE **Fig. 62** Study for *The Fence* 1986 pencil with touches of
pastel

Double portraits

I also find it very interesting to paint double portraits, in a way which is an extension of the eighteenth-century conversation piece rather than of the conventional portrait. A portrait of two people together (or even of a person with an animal) is also a portrait of the interaction between them. They react together – and, an incidental advantage, people are also more likely to forget the presence of the artist, or the camera, so they are less self-conscious. I particularly enjoy painting my daughters together: I find it fascinating to explore the relationship between the sisters, the likeness with a difference, subtle variations on a theme.

LEFT **Fig. 63** *Katie and Hannah Watching Television* 1986 pastel 38 × 56 cm/15 × 22 in
OVERLEAF **Fig. 64** *Katie and Hannah Watching Television* 1986 oil on board 33 × 48 cm/13 × 19 in

Two versions of the same situation. Neither of the girls was paying any attention to me. The oil painting started from the idea of two figures, at either end of the picture. In practice I could not make this work, so I used Katie's battered Snoopy to unite them. The pastel is less finished, but it seems to me the livelier and better portrait

Fig. 65 *Girls on the Beach* 1987 oil on board 36 × 50 cm/ 14 × 20 in. I have always liked painting pictures in which bits of activity are set against large, flat areas. Here this is translated into a sort of conversation piece. The portraiture is attempted through posture – Katle, the critical spectator; Hannah, all activity.

Action portraits

One of the enduring traditions in English art is that of the sporting picture, a very accessible form of expression. It is horse-racing that comes to mind first in this context, but there are examples of other sports. It is perhaps largely because racing is so intimately connected with money that it has assumed pride of place – plus the fact that George Stubbs, one of the great English painters, chose it as his principal subject. Incidentally, the many portraits of grooms, trainers and jockeys in his paintings are among the finest English portraits, and marvellous examples of the complete figure as portrait.

Pictures of sportsmen, and in particular of people involved in horse-racing, have occupied me for many years. Among the reasons I find sporting subjects so interesting is that they are so pictorial, so decorative, if you like. You have, for example, jockeys' colours, the club colours of footballers, and all the paraphernalia of the track and arena – which is so useful in composition. Then, as well as the pictorial aspects, you have the physical and psychological characteristics of the players. I am particularly intrigued by the way character is demonstrated in competitive interaction, under stress. Finally, there is the fascination of trying to combine the distinctive action of sport with a portrait of an individual.

Fig. 66 *Jimmy Greaves* 1966 acrylic on paper 38 × 28 cm/15 × 11 in. This portrait was one of a series commissioned by *The Sunday Times*.

OPPOSITE **Fig. 67** *Sketch of a Jockey* 1987 oil on board 36 × 25 cm/ 14 × 10 in

Fig. 68 *Owners and Trainers* 1984 a study in pen and ink and watercolour

THE FIGURE

James Horton

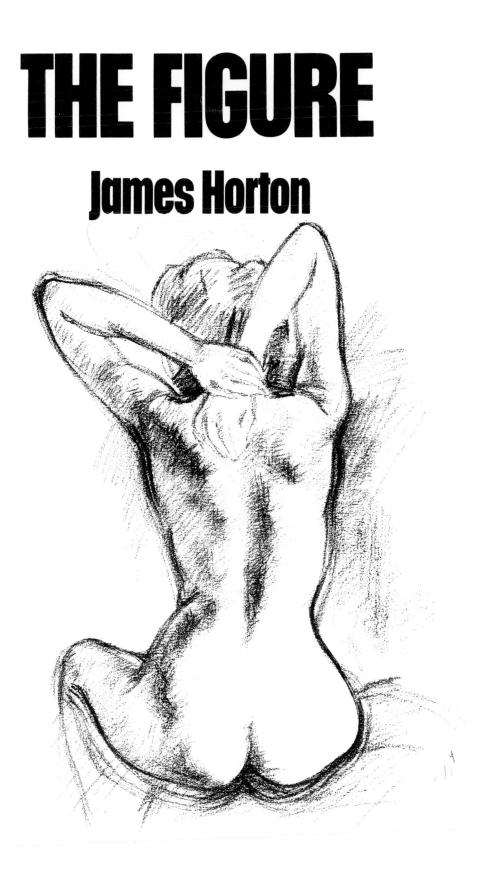

PORTRAIT OF AN ARTIST
JAMES HORTON

Fig. 1 James Horton working in his studio in Cambridge

James Horton was born in London where all of his education took place. His father, George Horton, was for many years a stonemason. Apart from carving marble and, more often, granite, he possessed a keen interest in painting and drawing, which sparked off in James the original desire to be an artist. The first serious considerations of making art a career came in his early teens, and at sixteen he felt confident enough to leave school in favour of going straight to art school.

For two years he studied drawing and painting at the Sir John Cass School of Art under Vivian Pitchforth and Percy Horton, the latter forming the strongest influence on his art and character. It was Percy Horton's integrity, love and understanding of great drawings, imparted through careful and enthusiastic teaching, that has been the backbone of James Horton's art since those early days.

On leaving the Cass School of Art he went on to study at City & Guilds School of Art for four years where he found a very sympathetic environment. It was a small art school which favoured working from life and figurative art in general. During this period James Horton also spent a good deal of time working upon figurative sculpture and before going on to the Royal College of Art for three years he was awarded a scholarship to Florence to study the Renaissance painters and sculptors.

Whilst at the RCA James Horton's work was included in the Young Contemporaries exhibition and he was a prizewinner in the BEA (British European Airways) Art Awards held at the Institute of Contemporary Art in the Mall, London. Since leaving the Royal College he has exhibited widely in Britain and abroad, including at the Royal Academy summer

68

Fig. 2 James Horton working from a model in his studio

shows and the Royal Portrait Society. He has staged six one-man shows which have been held in major capitals such as London, Stockholm and Dublin. In 1980 he was elected to the Royal Society of British Artists where each year he exhibits at least one large canvas as well as several smaller ones.

James Horton's paintings vary in size enormously from the small, freshly painted landscapes or figure studies always made from life, to the large figurative subjects which take many months to plan and execute.

As a writer he has published articles regularly since 1978 for *The Artist* magazine. This in turn led to him being invited to participate as one of the artist advisers on methods and materials at the hugely successful 'Paint & Painting' exhibition staged by Winsor & Newton in conjunction with the Tate Gallery in 1982.

As well as drawing and painting, the other great love in James Horton's life is music. As a classical guitarist he has both taught and given performances, the most recent being as part of the Cambridge Festival in 1982. Like many other artists he feels a great affinity with music, and when time permits enjoys spending many hours practising in order to improve his technique and repertoire.

Perhaps acknowledging an early debt to the teaching of Percy Horton, James Horton is now a known and respected teacher of art, finding inspiration for his own work from his students. He lives in Cambridge, which he finds a stimulating centre, and is a part-time lecturer at the Cambridge College of Arts and Technology. He is also a part-time lecturer at the Sir John Cass School of Art and visiting lecturer to the Mary Ward Centre in London.

WHAT EQUIPMENT DO YOU NEED?

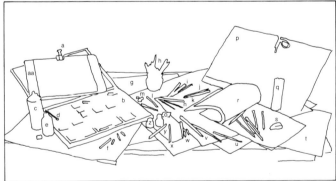

Fig. 3 Equipment for drawing with pastels, chalks, pencil, charcoal, coloured pencils, pen and ink, with key

a	bulldog clip	**j**	charcoal pencil	coloured Ingres
aa	small drawing board	**k**	general purpose	papers
b	box of Artist's Soft		pencil	**s** eraser
	Pastels	**l**	process chalk holder	**t** sketchbook
c	aerosol fixative	**m**	natural red chalk	**u** quill pen
d	spray		with holder	**v** reed pens
e	spray fixative	**n**	charcoal sticks	**w** Osmiroid pen with
f	conté process chalks	**o**	putty rubber	detachable nibs
g	assorted papers	**p**	portfolio	**x** dip pen
h	pastel pencils	**q**	coloured pencils	**y** Rotring drawing pen
i	graphite pencils	**r**	pad of Fabriano	**z** drawing inks

The basic requirements for making a drawing are quite simple and need only be a pencil and a sheet of paper. However, this is a rather limiting combination and sooner or later most people want to investigate and experiment with different types of media.

It might seem, from looking at **figs. 3 and 4**, that an enormous amount of equipment is required, but although some of this is basic and necessary to begin work, by no means does anyone learning to draw need all that is illustrated here straightaway. It has taken me some time to accumulate this equipment, which I use continuously in my work. To start with, the best thing to do might be to invest in the medium you find most appealing.

The question of quality is always difficult because it invariably relates to finance. As a professional artist, one should always use the best-quality equipment available, but it is really up to each individual to acquire the materials he or she can afford. For beginners usually the cheapest range available is adequate until some headway is made. Most paints (oil, acrylic and watercolour) come in two types:

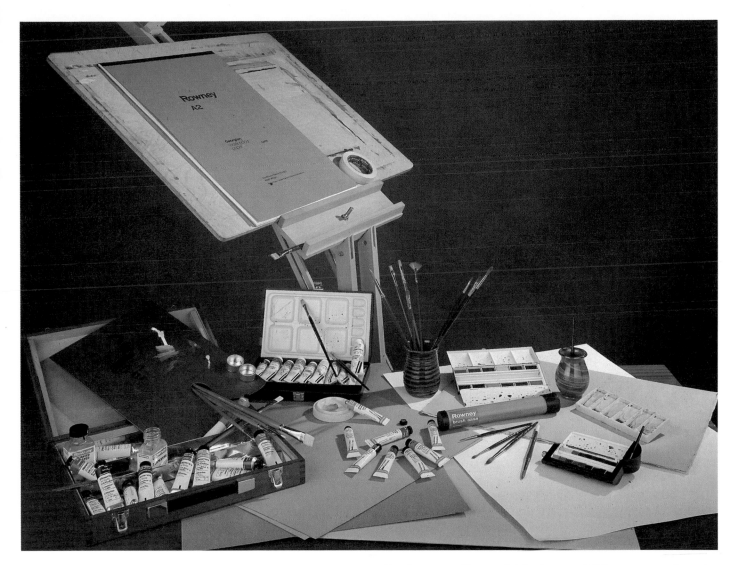

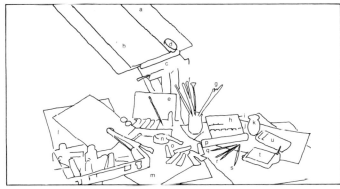

Fig. 4 Equipment for drawing with acrylic, watercolour, oil and gouache, with key

a A1 drawing board
b A2 watercolour pad
c Norwich radial easel
d masking tape
e acrylic paint box
f nylon brushes
g sable brushes
h studio watercolour box
i heavy watercolour paper

j hand-made watercolour paper
k water pot
l basic oil painting set
m selection of coloured papers
n china paint well
o gouache paints
p brush case
q best-quality sable

watercolour brush
r cheaper sable watercolour brushes
s nylon watercolour brush
t portable watercolour box incorporating water container
u large china paint well

Student quality, which has additives to make the colour go further and which is not as permanent as better-quality paint; and Artist quality, which in most cases is made with the highest-quality raw materials. This, of course, is reflected in the price. There is also a difference in the handling quality of the various grades of materials. Sable brushes perform better than synthetic; Artist quality colours are stronger than Student quality ones; and cheap paper will yellow and go brittle. It may take some time to build up to professional-quality materials, but ultimately every serious student should aim to achieve this.

One of the most basic pieces of equipment is an easel. It is possible to manage without one by propping a sketchbook or board on your knees, but anything larger than half imperial will be too cumbersome. The easel illustrated in **fig. 4** is sturdy, will take a very large drawing board and can be tilted back when watercolour paints are used.

It's a good idea to have two watercolour boxes. The small one illustrated is designed to slip in a pocket and has a water pot attached, which makes it convenient for carrying around. I usually have mine in my pocket whether I expect to be working or not. The bigger box is for more involved work and is suitable for mixing larger washes in conjunction with the china paint wells. You can choose your own colours to fill an empty box, but for general purposes the ready-fitted versions contain a perfectly adequate selection for beginners.

Brushes for watercolour need not be expensive. Sable brushes are the best but they are not cheap. However, since the introduction of brushes made of better-quality synthetic imitations of the sable fibre, such as the Dalon brush, there are now excellent alternatives available which are used by professionals and amateurs alike. If you choose sable, one medium- to large-size good-quality brush will suffice for most purposes, but if this is not within your price range, three synthetic brushes, sizes 2, 6 and 11, would be perfectly adequate. Nylon brushes seem to work well with gouache and acrylic paints, and often the longer-handled versions are preferable.

Care of brushes is essential, regardless of price. Never push down hard on the brush when rinsing in a water pot; this damages the hairs. Never let acrylic and oil paint dry on the brush, although watercolour and gouache are easily removed by soaking. A brush case is a good way of protecting your valued brushes.

The oil paint box illustrated in **fig. 4** is a standard set which includes brushes, a palette and a basic range of colours. You can buy oils separately but a ready-put-together box such as this one would be ideal. You will also need a palette to mix upon, some turpentine and linseed oil to mix with the paint, and a palette knife for removing unwanted paint from either the palette or the painting surface.

As with other media, pastels come in a range of standard colours, but unlike other media these are then graded into between six and eight tints. This is because pastels do not mix like paints and to achieve precise colours a greater range is necessary (see **fig. 3**). Smaller sets, sometimes with groups of colours put together by the manufacturer and suitable for portraits, figures or landscape, are also available. Pastel pencils are fun to use but do not have the covering power of ordinary pastels, nor are they made in such a large range of colours.

Like pastels, coloured pencils cannot be mixed in the same way as paints. However, the type of drawings made with these pencils (see **figs. 28-33**) usually do not aim at the same effect as that achieved with pastels or paints. A set of twenty-four coloured pencils (**fig. 3**) is sufficient.

The term 'pen and ink' covers an almost inexhaustible range if one includes the more commercial pens like biros and felt tips (see page 101). A technical drawing pen and Osmiroid Fountain Pen are very useful for

carrying around in a top pocket or bag, but the traditional dip pens, such as the quill, reed and steel nib pen, need to be used with open bottles of ink.

There are many different types of chalk available, all of which are processed in some way except the natural red-earth *sanguine*. This possesses a lovely feel, but processed chalk has its own qualities, such as flat edges which are useful for creating certain effects. It also comes in different grades. As far as I know, *sanguine* is no longer available in Britain, but it can be obtained in Italy.

To erase part of any chalk, charcoal or pastel drawing, a putty rubber will be needed. This is a soft, pliable piece of rubber which can be kneaded into any shape, and rather than rubbing out, the technique is to lift off by dabbing gently. For pencils use an ordinary eraser. Fixative can be obtained in aerosol form or a bottle with a spray diffuser. The latter is useful in case you ever experiment with making up your own fixative from recipes.

The paper shown in these photographs ranges from cartridge to watercolour and is of course only a small selection of what is available. Roughly speaking, each medium has a paper to which it is probably best suited, although there are no hard and fast rules. The choice of paper depends very much on personal preference.

Pastel works best on coloured papers – Fabriano Ingres is particularly suitable – so that dark and, more importantly, light colours can be seen easily. This is also true of oil, acrylic and gouache paints. Coloured papers such as Whatman and Fabriano are suitable for these paints. For oil paint the paper must be sized to prevent the oil soaking into it. It is always a good idea to stretch the paper first by soaking it for about five minutes, laying it flat upon a board and taping it down with gumstrip, which needs water to activate the glue. This cannot be done with self-adhesive tape. As the paper dries, it contracts and any wrinkles will pull tight and disappear. This procedure also applies to all the watercolour papers, although often with the heavier grades (from 90 lb upwards) the weight of the paper is sufficient to keep it flat.

Chalks in combination with white can also be used on coloured papers. Ink works best on better-quality cartridge paper, which is fairly smooth, and coloured pencils are probably best used on white or cream papers. Ordinary pencil can be used on any paper provided it is not too dark. Not essential but useful is a portfolio for either keeping new paper in or storing drawings.

One of the great values of learning to draw is to understand the medium being used. Once familiarity with it is gained, along with the improvement of your objective faculties, it is then a good time to explore another medium and a new way of expressing ideas.

POSING THE MODEL

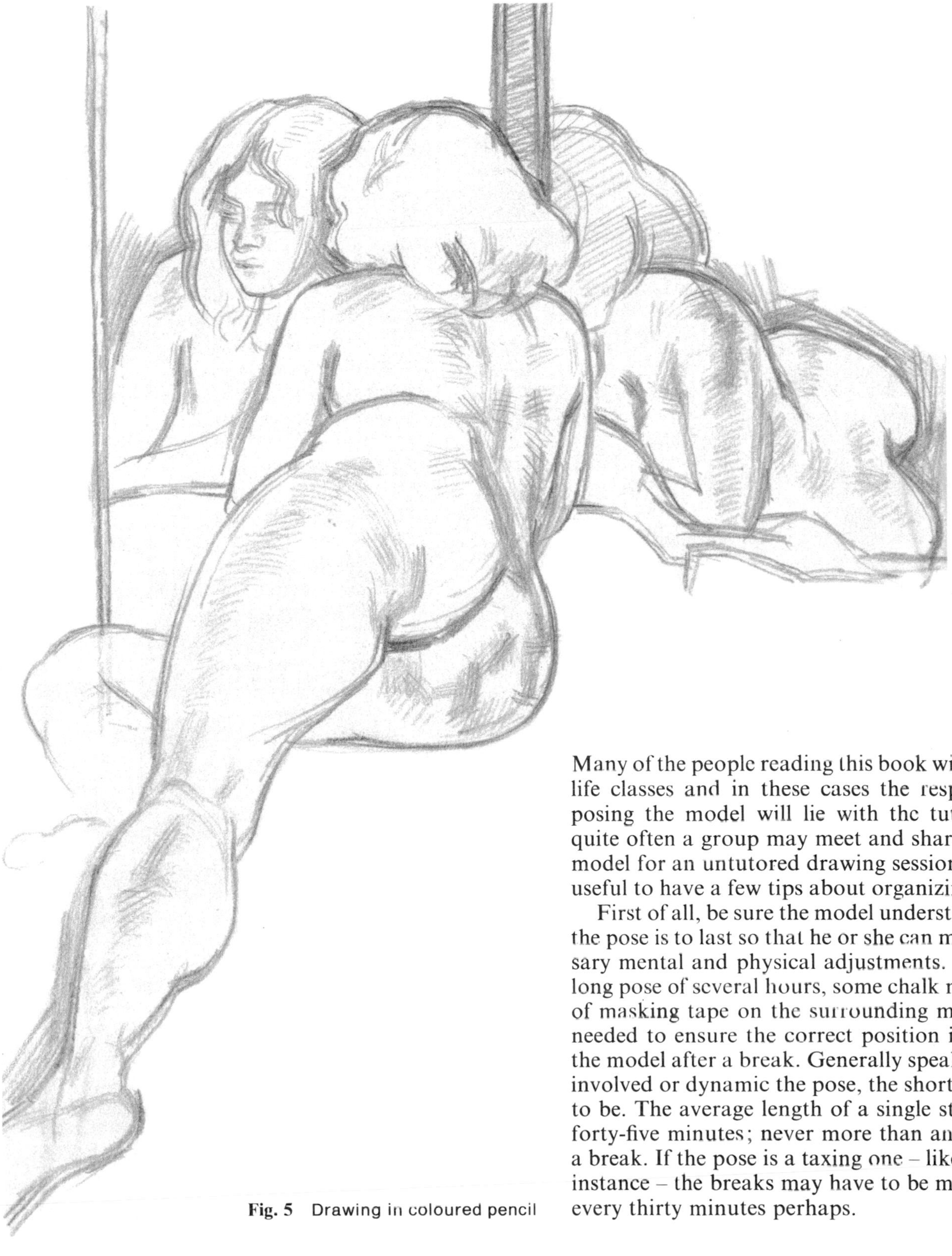

Many of the people reading this book will be attending life classes and in these cases the responsibility for posing the model will lie with the tutor. However, quite often a group may meet and share the cost of a model for an untutored drawing session, so it may be useful to have a few tips about organizing the class.

First of all, be sure the model understands how long the pose is to last so that he or she can make the necessary mental and physical adjustments. If it is to be a long pose of several hours, some chalk marks or strips of masking tape on the surrounding material will be needed to ensure the correct position is taken up by the model after a break. Generally speaking, the more involved or dynamic the pose, the shorter it may have to be. The average length of a single stretch is about forty-five minutes; never more than an hour without a break. If the pose is a taxing one – like standing, for instance – the breaks may have to be more frequent – every thirty minutes perhaps.

Fig. 5   Drawing in coloured pencil

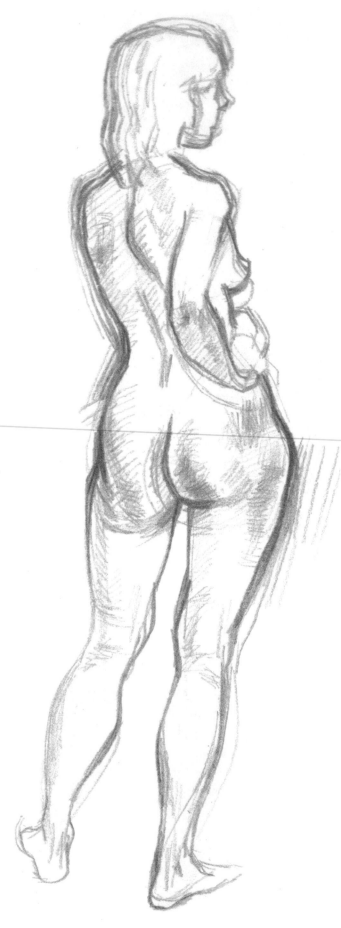

A word of caution about standing poses. If a model says that he or she is becoming uncomfortable, stop work immediately and let the model rest. I have known models to be perfectly all right one minute and to faint the next.

If possible, a number of props such as a studio couch, stool, or anything which will support the figure in a variety of positions is helpful. A selection of coloured drapes can be useful to have around, too, either to make the pose more comfortable for the model or simply to provide some immediate background.

Earlier I mentioned the necessity for the model to make the mental and physical adjustments for each pose. Once the model is settled it is the artist's turn to make the same adjustments. If it is possible to do so, walk around the model and size up the different possibilities that each viewpoint gives. Some poses may be quite dull from one position but very exciting from another, and this, of course, will have a lot to do with the lighting. Never accept what happens to be the pose from your immediate location. It is important to be selective about this so that your drawing begins with a good amount of enthusiasm and not a matter-of-fact acceptance.

Consider also the effects of different eye levels. If the model is posed on the floor and the artist is standing at an easel, some very interesting downward views will result. Conversely, if the model is posed on a throne or raised platform, as is often the case in an art school life room, everything will be much closer to the eye level, especially if you sit down.

If the room that you are drawing in is small or crowded, it may not be possible to choose a more advantageous position and in that case the discipline of coping with a pose over which there is no control can be a stimulating experience.

The length of the pose may vary from session to session, but most classes or groups will want some short poses at some stage (by short, I mean anything from one to ten minutes). This can be rather disconcerting to some people, particularly the inexperienced or less confident, because of the speed in drawing required. However, these shorter poses are an essential part of learning to draw, and later in the book I will discuss the value of drawing from moving models such as dancers and people in workout classes, which also demands swift execution.

The main point to remember when drawing rapidly is that you are not after a finished drawing but an image that captures the essence of the pose. One advantage of short poses, of course, is that you can ask your model to adopt more dynamic positions which would be impossible to hold for long periods.

Fig. 6 Drawing in coloured pencil

STARTING A DRAWING

Fig. 7 Five- and
ten-minute poses in ink

It has often been said that 'all beginnings are difficult' and this was never more true than of beginning a drawing. The best tactic, I always feel, is to use the ploy adopted when going swimming: instead of creeping in an inch at a time – jump in! But before doing so one or two things ought to be considered: the length of the pose, the size of paper, and the type of medium to be used. For instance, if a sketchbook of A4 size is to be used, thick charcoal or pastels are probably not a good idea because they will saturate the drawing area very quickly. Conversely, a thin HB pencil used on an Imperial sheet of paper could also cause problems, mainly because it will take a long time to build up an image of any density. However, both these combinations are quite feasible in certain circumstances: the charcoal and sketchbook could be employed in a short 'gesture' drawing of two or three minutes, for example, and the larger format with pencil could be used with a pose of several hours which would sustain gradual building up.

One other aspect that ought to be considered before beginning is the image size, by which I mean literally the size of your drawing upon the paper. In order to understand the sort of rhythms that occur in a pose it is essential to draw the whole figure, so work out roughly in advance how much of the paper the drawing will occupy and be sure it is enough to include all of the model.

One way of getting a life drawing session started and at the same time overcoming the initial tentative beginnings is to draw a series of five- and ten-minute poses such as in **fig. 7**. This has the advantage of forcing you to make marks within a limited time scale, and after a while the adrenaline begins to flow which helps to overcome inhibitions about the results.

The full value of drawing short poses can only be realized if the *whole* pose is drawn. To spend ten minutes on developing just a head and shoulders, for example, means that the rate of drawing is the same as for a longer pose. The discipline of a short pose is to force the artist to make a statement, complete in itself, about the pose given within the allotted time. This way your thinking process has to speed up to deal with the urgency of the situation.

Measuring

This brings me on to measuring, which is essential at some stage in a drawing in order to keep a check on proportions. However, it is very easy to let measuring become a method of construction rather than of checking. I always do a substantial amount of drawing before I measure so that I can check the proportions of one part against another. Certainly a drawing can be made by measuring before each statement and gradually building up a tight network of inter-related marks, but the drawbacks are that it rather inhibits the 'jumping in' approach and, ironically, it is also easy to become inaccurate by making a slight miscalculation which is magnified each time a measurement is made. It is rather better to trust your eye a little more and to measure the larger parts of the figure, such as the distance from the pit of the neck to the pubic arch and the pubic arch to the feet. To try and measure how many times the head goes into the body, for example, would almost certainly result in inaccuracy because of the many times the pencil (used for measuring) is moved.

Figs. 8, 10 and 11 show the sort of distances on a figure that are useful to measure and then compare to other parts of the body. For instance, in **fig. 11** the distances from head to shoulder and shoulder to waist are exactly the same. The same distance divided into the length from the waist to the heel goes about four times. **Figs. 8 and 10** show areas of the body roughly divided, at fairly obvious points, for comparison.

There is one other aid which can be used while drawing and that is a plumb line. This is exactly the same as the type that builders use on site and it serves the same purpose – to ascertain a true vertical. A plumb line is easily made by attaching a weight to a piece of string about two or three feet long. When held against the figure it will show which parts of the body correspond to the same vertical line. It is particularly useful in standing poses.

Obtaining a true horizontal can be more of a problem. It is easiest if you are sitting on an art school-type 'donkey' – a low wooden bench which you sit astride and which has a support at the front for leaning your board against. By lowering your eye to the top edge of your board you will get a true horizontal. Otherwise hold up a pencil and ensure it is as horizontal as possible.

Figs. 9 and 12 show the use of verticals and horizontals when measuring. In **fig. 9** the knee lines up with the armpit, although in space it is a lot further away. The horizontals in **fig. 12** are very useful for making sure that the figure occupies the correct place in space and perspective. It is very easy to misjudge the relation of the feet to the head in reclining poses unless this sort of check is made.

Proportion

One hears the word proportion quite a lot within the context of figure drawing. Generally speaking, it refers to the way in which various parts of the body, often the limbs, relate to each other. Proportions differ quite considerably between individuals and often the key to achieving something of the character of the model will be in getting the proportions right. Sometimes measuring will help, but often it is better to try to use your eye to determine the rough proportional characteristics. This is one very good reason for making sure the whole figure is included when drawing standing models, because without their length it is impossible to know their width! Quite often I have seen drawings in the life room which in themselves are of a passable standard but when compared to the model do not have the right proportional characteristics.

Exercise Using a plumb line and a horizontal make a drawing from a three-hour pose. Plot carefully the parts of the figure which correspond to the verticals and horizontals. For the purposes of this exercise draw in all the construction lines so that when the drawing is complete it is possible to see clearly the parts of the figure which link up.

In addition, make some relative measurements as illustrated (**figs. 8, 10 and 11**) and as before include the construction lines.

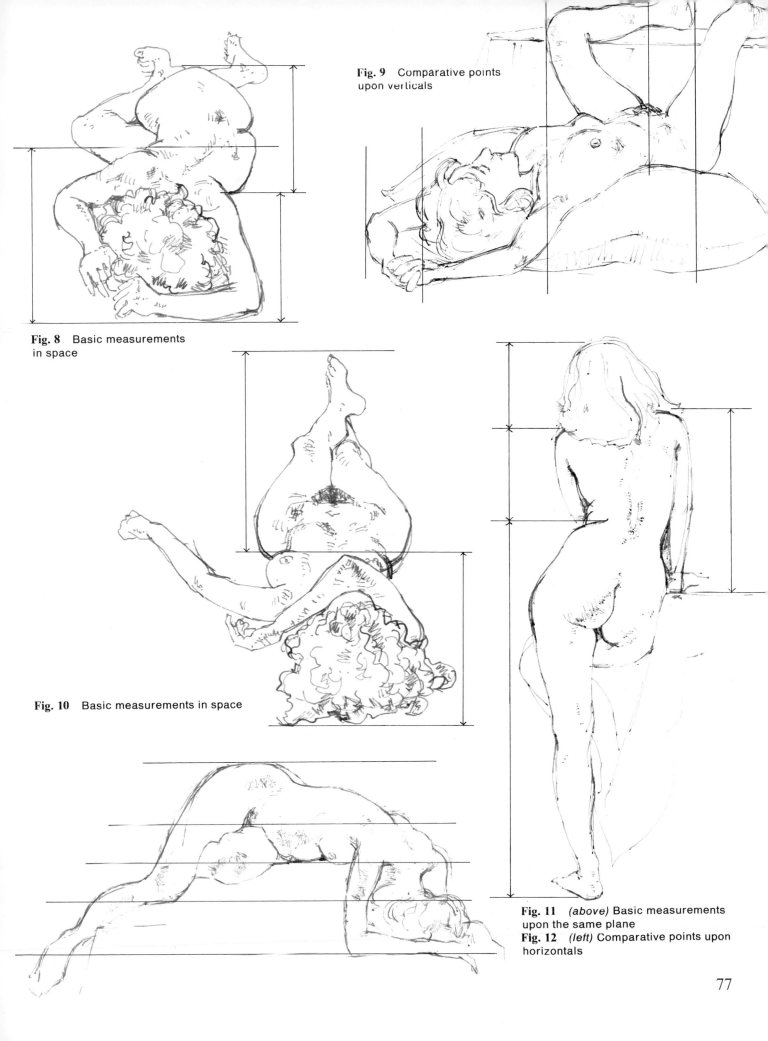

Fig. 9   Comparative points
upon verticals

Fig. 8   Basic measurements
in space

Fig. 10   Basic measurements in space

Fig. 11   *(above)* Basic measurements
upon the same plane
Fig. 12   *(left)* Comparative points upon
horizontals

77

BALANCE, SHAPE AND FORM

Fig. 13
Drawing in ink

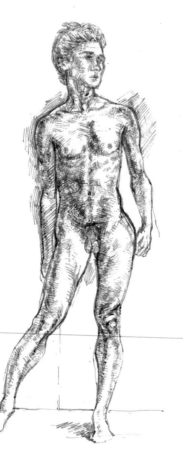

Fig. 14
Drawing in
coloured pencil

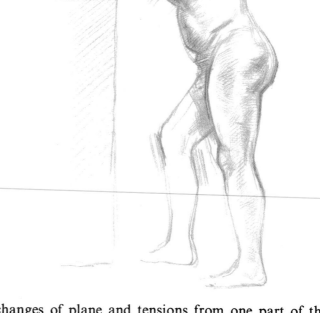

Having discussed the sort of things to be borne in mind when beginning a drawing, let us now consider some of the elements involved in a drawing once under way.

One of the first aspects that should be looked at is the shape of your model. Does she resemble the model in **fig. 15** or **fig. 17**? This could very easily affect the approach you make to the subject. It may seem a fairly obvious consideration, especially when the two examples are as extreme as they are in these cases, but there have been times when I have looked at a selection of drawings made by students in a life room and it was quite possible to believe they were all drawing a different model. To achieve the character of a person's shape is not as straightforward as one might think and cannot always be managed simply by making a number of measurements.

Form is a part of drawing that can be tackled in a variety of ways, depending upon either your approach or the character of the model. In **fig. 13** I found the structure of the model's body, being thin and without superficial fat, very suitable for making a more intricate and carefully studied drawing about precise

changes of plane and tensions from one part of the body to another. This contrasts sharply with **fig. 17** where the form is voluminous and to have worked into the drawing to the same degree would almost certainly have lost the rotund quality of the model.

Fig. 14 shows a fairly solidly built model without the generous curves of **fig. 17** but at the same time lacking the sinews and general thinness of **fig. 13**. In this drawing I found it rewarding to say something about the form contained between fairly strong contours. The fact that the pose was in profile was useful to show the grouping of the various parts of the contour and how they connected through to the other side of the body, in particular the area between the shoulder blade and chest, the stomach and back, and the top leg and buttock.

Balance is of the utmost importance in many poses, especially standing ones. **Figs. 14, 15 and 16** show a variety of ways in which balance can affect a drawing. In **fig. 15** the drawing explains itself well enough without any obvious additional supports. The angles across the breast and hips show that the weight of the

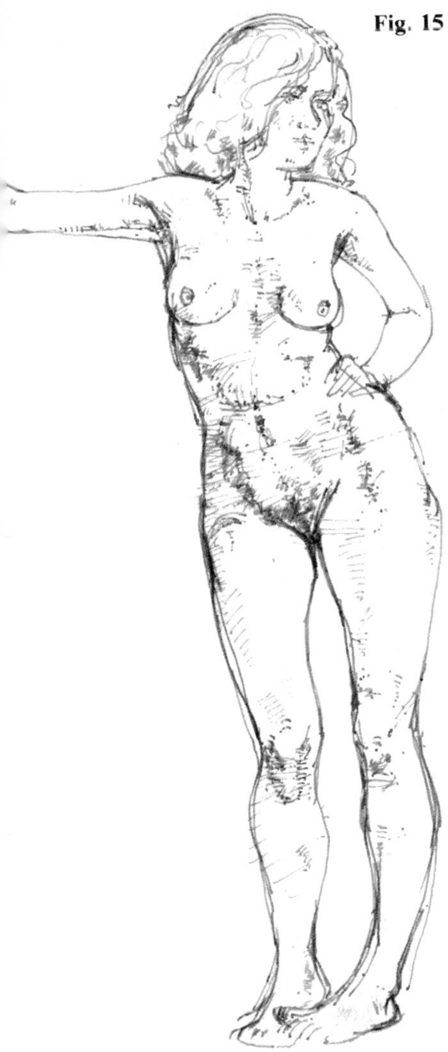

Fig. 15 Drawing in ink

Fig. 16 Drawing in coloured pencil

Fig. 17
Drawing in pencil

figure is supported outside its own sphere. Notice, too, the central axis between the pit of the neck and the pubic arch and the angle it makes. If the figure were supporting its own weight the mass of the torso would have to be directly over the weight-bearing leg. Notice the distance and perspective between the feet in **fig. 16** and how important it is to the stance that they should be included. Unless the feet are drawn in a standing pose the drawing will never balance properly.

Exercise Pose your model in a standing position with no support and make a drawing. Then pose the model leaning against a wall or supporting the weight in some way and observe the differences between the two. Remember to watch the centre line from the pit of the neck to the pubic arch or to follow the spine at the back to show the central axis. The angle through the nipples and pelvis will give firm indications of the weight distribution.

If possible, try to make some drawings of two very differently shaped models and make a note of how you find yourself treating each subject.

TONAL DRAWING

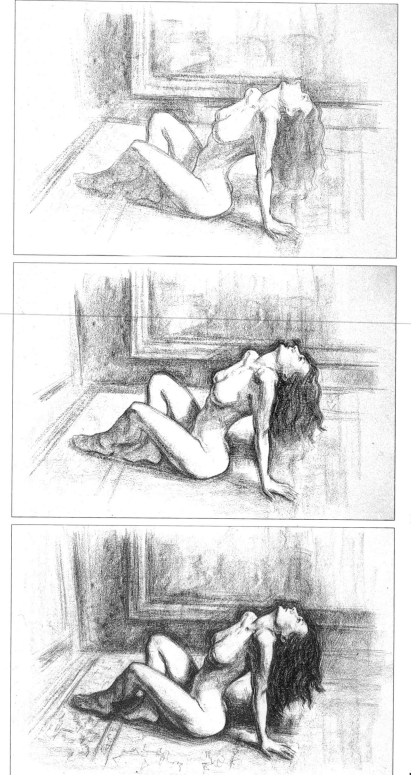

Fig. 18 First stage: drawing in black conté chalk

Fig. 19 Second stage

Fig. 20 Finished stage

Tonal drawing uses mass, i.e. shading, rather than just line. Before attempting any sort of tonal drawing it is important to select a light source that is suitable. On the whole, consistency of light is the best. Light that comes from one source only is particularly good because it gives clearly defined shadows. **Fig. 21** shows a figure standing in light from one source. Notice how the tone of the background, relative to whatever part of the figure it is seen against, has been used. This gives a value to the highlighted parts of the figure. Even though a background may be uniform in tone and surface, as soon as an object is placed in front of it the fall of light upon that object will make the background appear to vary tonally.

In the case of this drawing the background was a plain dark cloth, but when the figure was placed in front of it immediately some parts of her could be seen to be darker and some lighter. Most of her left side is darker than the background, for example, because it is in full shadow. Notice also the effect of reflected light: this usually shows up the edge upon a piece of form nearest the viewer; for example, in **fig. 21**, the right buttock, both the arms and the right leg.

To gain the most from a tonal drawing it is essential to understand relative tones as I have just described. Unlike a linear drawing, which can sit on a blank sheet of paper and not need any indication of background, a tonal drawing must be seen in relation to its immediate surroundings.

Using a sheet of textured watercolour paper and a piece of black chalk, **figs. 18-20** show how I envisaged making a drawing that would adequately describe form, using only tone.

First stage I made a very loose linear statement just to plot where the masses of tone should be. Once this was established, using the side of the chalk, I covered all those areas which were receiving at least some slight shadow. It can be seen that even at this early stage a pattern of tone is emerging due to the structure of the drawing with tone.

Second stage Working on top of the first tone, strength was given to areas like the hair and parts of the background to create further a tonal pattern. Major changes of plane upon the figure have also been drawn more carefully to establish solidity. Because of the direction of the light, which was strong and from above, shadows were inevitable, but within the context of a drawing like this they can be used to great advantage to assist both with the description of the form and the tonal pattern as a whole.

Finished stage As the drawing of the figure was now well established, some further enhancement of the tonal pattern was made and the development of texture in the hair and the area surrounding the face, shoulders, chest and right leg was increased. Notice how the palest tone on the right foot has remained constant, but how shadow areas around it have deepened. This illustrates how tones can be described relative to each other and to the whole. If little patches of tone of varying strength, instead of broad areas, had been put in from the beginning, the result might well have been disjointed.

Exercise Pose your model in a strong, consistent light source for three hours. Make a drawing which from the outset describes the subject with tone. Try not just to draw an outline and then fill it in; use the tone to construct the drawing. At the beginning put a light tone over every area that is not receiving direct light, then work systematically into that tone, darkening it where necessary. Pay attention to the tonal pattern and contrasts between light and dark.

Fig. 21
Drawing in
charcoal, pencil
and wash

LINEAR DRAWING

Fig. 22
'Kneeling Nude', in ink

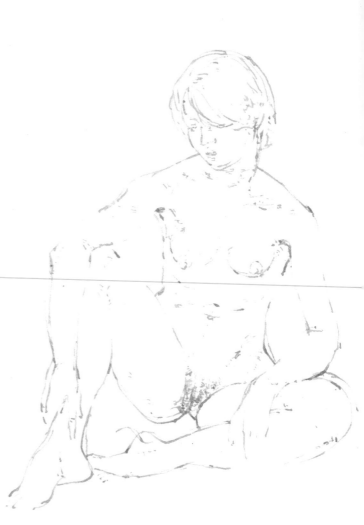

Fig. 23
'Seated Nude', in ink

Although one does not tend to think of the execution of drawings fitting neatly into compartments, when learning to draw it can be advantageous to break down the various methods of drawing in order to understand a specific process. When looking at drawings in museums, galleries or art books it is often possible to identify a particular approach. For instance, artists like Klimt and Schiele are well known for their linear drawings and Rembrandt for his rich and sombre shadows. In this section I would like to investigate linear drawing.

First, what exactly is meant by linear drawing? Quite simply, stating the case in line and not using tone or shadow. This does not mean, however, that the drawing should have nothing but a single line, like a tracing. On the contrary, it is still possible to make a drawing that indicates sufficient changes of plane and contains structure, yet is still within the limits of a linear drawing. As in the tonal section, where a drawing was constructed with tone, here we shall look at some drawings that deal only in linear concepts.

Breaking down the elements of drawing in this way can be very useful in strengthening the concept because the aim has been more singular. I find it a very helpful exercise to be forced into a positive frame of mind by electing to tackle a drawing in a specific way.

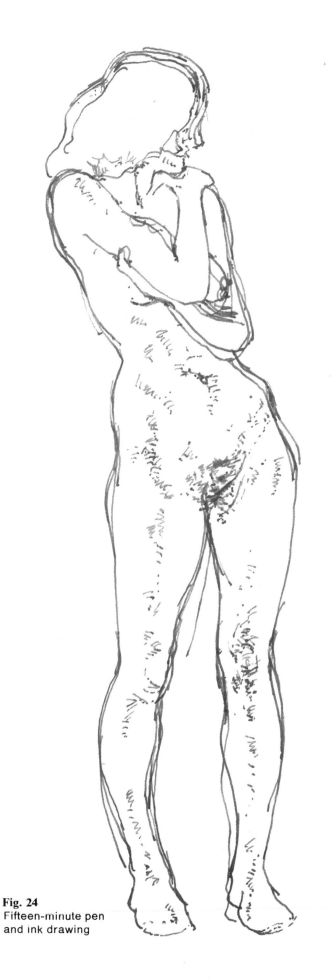

Fig. 24
Fifteen-minute pen
and ink drawing

Very often the decision to treat a drawing in a particular way can be determined by the available light. For instance, if the lighting is consistent and coming from one direction, as in the standing nude in **fig. 21**, a tonal drawing would be a good idea. However, very often the light can be diffuse or multi-directional, giving no clear shadows at all or, worse, shadows everywhere. In this case a linear drawing would be a good choice because the lighting as such could be ignored, enabling one to concentrate on linear rhythms and structure.

Although almost any medium can be used, I personally find pen and ink a very satisfying combination. **Fig. 22**, 'Kneeling Nude', and **fig. 23**, 'Seated Nude', were both made in twenty minutes, using a fountain pen in an A4 sketchbook. **Fig. 24** shows a pen drawing executed in roughly fifteen minutes. You will notice that as well as line there are statements about changes of plane. These I added to give the figure solidity and in fact they were not exactly added, but used as part of the construction. However, these marks are not sufficient to interfere with the flow of the line.

Although changes of plane have been stated, which give the figure a better feeling of solidity, there is still an indication as to the direction of light. In this case it does not matter and in fact would probably have served only to distract from the main conception had shadow areas been indicated. The quality of line is fundamentally what this drawing is about. In several parts of the figure it is possible to see just a single pen line and even in the multi-line areas the origin of the line was of 'first time right' quality. Only with linear drawing, and particularly ink, can that confident 'first time right' quality really be achieved. In order to obtain this, a line must be taken without interruption for as long as possible, and even if the line is not right it can be changed by overdrawing in the same fashion. In this way the nature of line can be understood and even if many lines arc made in one area they still add to the overall quality of the drawing.

As I stated earlier, the local conditions can often determine what manner of drawing is to be made. Very often poses of a short length (say, fifteen or twenty minutes) are ideal for linear drawing because the time scale does not permit a great deal of overwork. With a longer pose it is tempting to take the drawing beyond a linear statement and use tone and shadow areas.

Exercise Make several drawings in ink from poses of not more than twenty minutes. Be sure to include the whole figure. Try not to 'sketch' with the pen; take a line for as long as possible, without removing the pen from the paper. Look carefully at the model and draw confidently, paying particular attention to the quality and expressiveness of the line.

DRAWING WITH PENCIL

Fig. 25

Fig. 26   (right)

Fig. 27   (far right)

Perhaps the most standard method employed in drawing is pencil upon white cartridge paper. What we now call a lead pencil actually has no lead in it at all and consists largely of graphite. These pencils can be obtained in various grades, varying from extremely hard, which scarcely marks the paper at all, to very soft, which makes a very dark mark almost as black as charcoal. In the centre of this range is the **HB** pencil and the grades progress to 6B (soft) and 6H (hard) in each direction (see **fig. 3**). In most cases, for our purposes, the H range is seldom used; from HB onwards is the most usual.

Until some familiarity and basic facility in drawing is gained it is probably a good thing for a beginner to use the combination of pencil and cartridge paper as it

is relatively straightforward and does not demand the special thought required by many other media. On the whole I think it is better to use a slightly softer rather than harder grade of pencil as this gives more flexibility. With a softer pencil it is possible to press lightly for a sensitive line and harder for a dark line or shading, such as in the pencil drawings illustrated in **figs. 25-27**.

Paper is obviously an important consideration, whatever the medium employed, and apart from the permanence factor the choice of paper is largely personal regarding colour and texture. In my experience the majority of people prefer a paper which has a slight grain or texture to it as this gives some 'bite' to the pencil or crayon. However, pencil on smooth paper is often used when soft or smudged edges are needed.

DRAWING WITH COLOURED PENCILS

Fig. 28

Fig. 29

Most of the other media dealt with in this book are quite traditional in essence and have been around in some shape or form for many centuries. Wax-based coloured pencils, however, are a fairly recent development. Having started life as a medium for children, they are now in a more refined form widely used by artists and students.

These pencils are extremely flexible and can be used on almost any type of paper. Some very interesting and charming effects can be achieved by gradually building up a drawing with layer upon layer. If an effect of 'full colour' is to be aimed at, it is worth investing in a reasonable selection of a dozen or more coloured pencils. This is because their mixing potential is rather

Fig. 30

limited, unlike paint where just a few colours can be mixed into many combinations. It is therefore useful to have as wide a selection of colours as possible.

Although there cannot be said to be a right or a wrong way of using these pencils, in my experience I have found that a gradual building up using a cross-hatching type of technique can be very satisfactory.

Because of the colour, this medium has many possibilities that monochrome media do not possess. In **fig. 28** the pale, unbroken form of the model has been emphasized by sandwiching it between the crimson cushion and the orange-red hair. This contrast in colours helps the drawing a great deal. Although different colours have been used upon the figure this is more to describe the form rather than actual surface colour. For this drawing it was important not to crowd the figure with too much modelling otherwise the overall shape would have been lost.

Much the same is true of **fig. 30** where the colour of the hair has been increased even more than in **fig. 28**. The colours around the outside of the figure also play their part in making the pale, simple shape of the leg work.

Fig. 29 shows the delicate effect these pencils can achieve and also how the colour can be used in quite an inventive and almost decorative way. Rather than trying to imitate exactly the colours of the subject, as one would be inclined to do with paint, with coloured pencils it is an interesting idea to use colour to enhance the feeling of the drawing in a more personal way. In other words, you can deliberately choose colours which may not exist in the subject as such, but which work well within the context of the drawing.

Figs. 31-33 show the gradual development of an initial drawing that was made using several different coloured pencils, such as mauve for the body, brown and orange for the chair and green for the plant. I deliberately changed the colour periodically for no other reason than to keep the drawing alive. If I needed to redraw a part then using a fresh colour enabled me to see more clearly the new lines I was making.

First stage Having lightly sketched the basic form, the drawing developed with still no appreciable use of colour around the figure. Earlier I had decided the hair was not doing what I wanted it to so I asked the model to push one side back. As can be seen in this drawing this was much better because it showed the junction of neck to shoulder more clearly and also made a better design. This is one of the few situations where I would advocate the use of erasing. Having decided that an area like this is unsuitable, to erase it becomes essential. This is not the same, however, as rubbing out every 'wrong' line that is made because these are a necessary part of the growth of a drawing.

Second stage At this point more colour was added, not only around the figure to the chair, cushion and plant, but to the figure itself, further defining the changes of plane and general drawing. The image has also become denser.

Finished stage Between this and the previous stage I had second thoughts about the head and erased a part in order to redraw it. The interesting aspect about a drawing done in this manner is that it becomes difficult to know when to stop. By the time the drawing had reached this stage I felt that the figure was quite well resolved and the amount of background sufficient to make an interesting study. There were parts which I felt could have taken more work, but much of the charm of this medium lies in its sketchy, rather unfinished quality. This drawing had already become substantially more worked than any of the others and I felt that it contained enough substance for me to stop working on it.

Fig. 31 *(above right)* First stage

Fig. 32 *(right)* Second stage

Fig. 33 *(opposite)* Finished stage

DRAWING WITH CHARCOAL

Fig. 34

One tends to associate this medium with large, black, often rather messy drawings, and certainly charcoal is ideal for more expressive, forceful drawing; but it is also excellent for smaller, more controlled work. For me, charcoal is one of the most sensitive and responsive media and I find it capable of being used in most situations.

The usual way to buy charcoal is in a box which contains a number of sticks about 6 inches long. The thickness varies from about $\frac{1}{2}$ inch to roughly the thickness of an ordinary pencil. Indeed, it is possible to obtain charcoal in the form of a pencil, which can provide a more convenient method of using it.

Because charcoal is such a versatile medium it is possible to keep a drawing on the go for a long time without it becoming overworked. Unlike many other media, charcoal, being particularly soft, lies rather like a powder on the surface of the paper, which makes it easy to lift off with a putty rubber. It is also possible to smudge and soften edges from dark tones into light. Quite often this can be done with a stump, which is basically paper bound tightly into the shape of a thick pencil, but many artists prefer to use their fingers and this is certainly just as effective.

This was the case in **fig. 34**, a large drawing (30×20 inches) made with the thickest piece of charcoal. Here I used my fingers a great deal to soften the edges of tones. Making drawings this size is enormously satisfying in many ways, not least being the feeling of greater physical involvement. One tends to use the whole arm much more to make marks rather than just the wrist as in smaller works. When working on this scale it is very important to remember to stand back constantly in order to observe the reduced image size. This is essential otherwise all manner of proportional errors will arise. Because the image size is so large it is necessary to get far enough away to reduce the image on the retina to the equivalent of an A4 sketchbook at arm's length. Drawings of this sort are best executed standing at an easel where it is easier to step back.

In contrast to this, and using the smallest-size piece of charcoal, are **figs. 35 and 36**, both of which are roughly a quarter of the size of **fig. 34**. In order to avoid unwanted smudging of smaller drawings, a good tactic is to support the hand by pivoting upon the little finger. This serves the additional function of keeping the palm off the drawing.

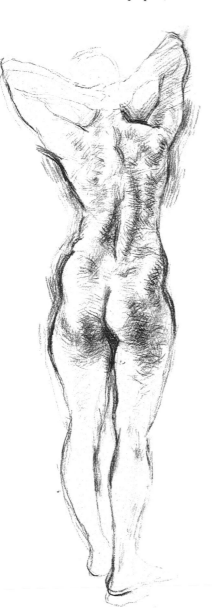

Fig. 35

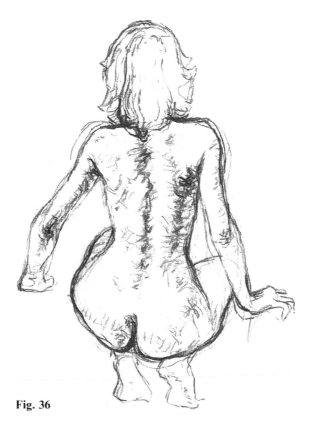

Fig. 36

91

DRAWING WITH CHALKS

Fig. 37
Drawing in red-earth
sanguine

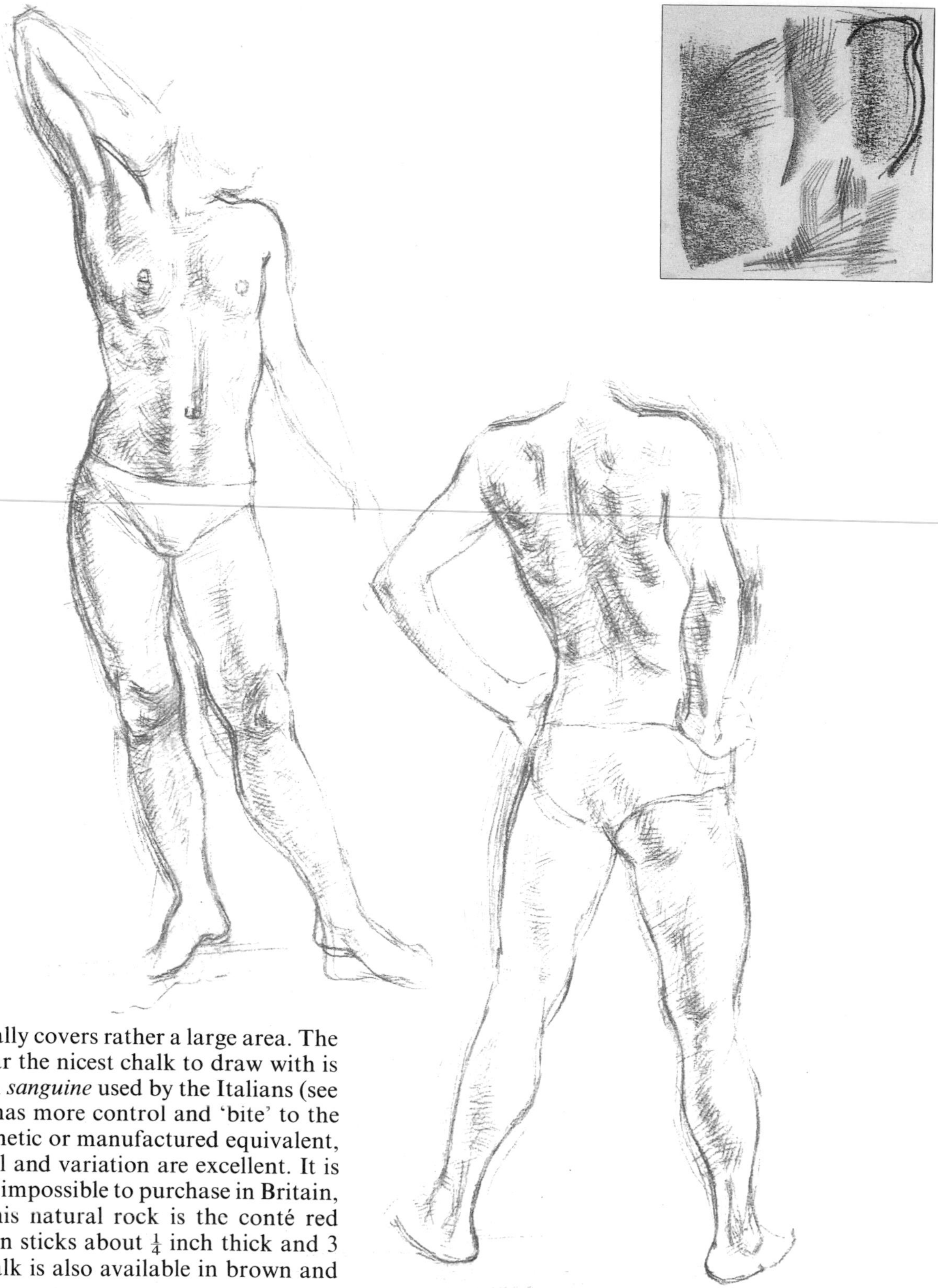

The term chalk actually covers rather a large area. The traditional and by far the nicest chalk to draw with is the natural red-earth *sanguine* used by the Italians (see **fig. 37**). This chalk has more control and 'bite' to the paper than any synthetic or manufactured equivalent, and its linear control and variation are excellent. It is now, sadly, virtually impossible to purchase in Britain, but derived from this natural rock is the conté red chalk which comes in sticks about $\frac{1}{4}$ inch thick and 3 inches long. The chalk is also available in brown and

black, but of the three, the red is the softest. When used upon paper with a textured surface conté is particularly good for designing large areas of tone because it can be turned on to its flat side and dragged across the paper, as in **fig. 38** which uses black conté. The drawing in **fig. 39**, also in black conté chalk, was made on high-quality textured paper, giving a very satisfying 'bite' to the chalk.

Because of its softness it can be difficult to maintain a reasonable point on this type of chalk. There are two methods of doing this: one is to use the edge of a freshly broken piece of chalk, often quite sharp, although it can feel a little odd drawing with one side of a cube; the other is simply to sharpen the chalk to a point with a knife. **Fig. 40**, in brown conté chalk, demonstrates the chalk used on its side as in **fig. 38**, but in conjunction with lines as shading. For this I had two pieces of chalk: one with a sharpened point and the other without.

When using the natural rock, it is essential to place it in a chalk holder and scrape it into shape. Although designed for use without, it is possible to use any processed chalk in a holder if desired. However, this would restrict the use of the side of the chalk as just described.

Fig. 38 and
Fig. 39 *(far right)*
Drawings in
black conté chalk

Like charcoal, it is possible to obtain chalk in a pencil form and this can be very useful for making a more detailed type of drawing where a consistent point is necessary. **Fig. 41** was drawn in blue chalk pencil, heightened with white. When used upon a toned paper it is possible to use white chalk as a highlight, but I always feel this should be done sparingly – a little can be very effective and contribute to the structure of the drawing, but too much can look as if snow has fallen!

One method of giving increased sensitivity to the chalk pencil is to dampen the paper first with a sponge and draw into the damp surface (see **fig. 42**). Any mistakes can be wiped out with the sponge, although the advantage of this technique is that they are not removed entirely and a ghost of the image remains, as a guide to making a new line. **Fig. 43** was done in exactly the same way as **fig. 42** but using the sponge deliberately to make tones. For this technique heavyweight paper is best because thinner papers can begin to disintegrate during rubbing with the sponge.

Fig. 40   *(above)* Drawing in brown conté chalk

Fig. 41   *(left)* Drawing in blue chalk pencil

Fig. 42   *(right)* and **Fig. 43** *(far right)*
Drawings in chalk pencil on dampened surface

DRAWING WITH PASTELS

Fig. 44   (right)

Fig. 45   (opposite)

96

Pastels are, of course, in essence similar to chalks. Their composition is very simple – pigment with a small amount of binding medium. They have good covering power and are produced in a wide range of colours from the very darkest to lightest tints. Being fully opaque, pastels are highly suited to working on toned paper. In fact, their great charm is probably not fully realized unless used on a coloured ground.

Although a finished pastel can resemble an oil painting in density, the approach and application are very different. In the eighteenth century many portraits were made in pastels and were very polished in effect, with all edges softened by a stump or smudged with a finger. They were actually done in direct imitation of oil paintings. However, since Edgar Degas (1834–1917) we tend to think of pastels rather differently and as a medium of great individuality.

When painting one tends to use anything between half a dozen and a dozen colours but seldom more. With these colours many combinations are possible by mixing two, three or four colours together and thus achieving a mix of exactly the hue desired.

With pastels, however, the technique is to have many colours of varying tints – ready-mixed, in fact. Some pastelists work with up to two hundred different tints. Pastels can be mixed or blended either with the fingertip or with cotton wool, but there does come a time, however, when the surface of the paper becomes saturated and will not take any more pigment unless it is fixed.

There is another approach. Rather than trying to mix or blend an exact colour, as in painting, an optical effect can be achieved by laying one colour over another (see **fig. 44**). By building up in this way a little of each colour shows through, rather in the form of a mesh. This technique is much closer to actual drawing because of the nature of drawing individual lines – stroke by stroke.

Obviously there cannot be said to be a correct or incorrect way of handling pastels, or any other medium for that matter. The approach must always rest with the individual. Some experimentation is useful to discover a way of working that is in harmony with the aims and objectives of each person.

Fig. 46 First stage

Fig. 47 *(above)* Second stage
Fig. 48 *(opposite)* Finished stage

Figs. 46-48 show the development of a drawing in pastels.

First stage Using a neutral grey sheet of Ingres paper I began the drawing with a black pastel. The composition was high on the list of priorities as well as blocking out the rough drawing of the figure. Once the figure seemed to be working on the page, I used one or two bright colours, such as Lemon Yellow tint 0 and Yellow Ochre tint 0, to indicate some high points on the back and establish the major changes of plane.

Second stage Colour was introduced here, applied fairly evenly so that no single part received too much attention. Using the stroke by stroke technique, the build-up continued, using Burnt Sienna, Red Grey, Burnt Umber, Reddish Purple and other suitable flesh tints, placing them side by side. At this stage I was aware that some of the colours, especially on the figure, were rather bright. However, as will be seen in the subsequent development, these areas were worked over with some patches left to show through.

Finished stage Apart from the addition of an extra pot on the window ledge, most of the work centred around getting the figure finally into shape. The con-

tours have now been lost completely and colour has taken over. Some of the bright orange and mauve colours on the back were tempered and worked into the general form. At no time was any mark rubbed out. If I felt a part was incorrect or needed adjusting, I did it by adding colour either over the top or placing some colour adjacent to the offending area to alter its relative effect.

At the end of this pastel the surface was just about saturated and ready for fixing. When a pastel has reached this stage it is generally advisable to fix it, especially if work is to continue, because there is a limit to how much the surface can hold before the pigment begins to fall off as powder. If a pastel is framed under glass immediately it is complete, then fixing is not necessarily essential.

There is much debate about the alteration of a finished pastel that can occur after fixing. Some alteration, sadly, is inevitable because in covering the loose particles of pigment with a liquid the optical effect of the medium is changed. However, unless framed straightaway, some fixing is needed or smudging is certain to occur. I would recommend that some experimenting with different types of fixative should be made because certain solutions act differently upon various papers.

DRAWING WITH INK

For a beginner, the prospect of drawing from life with ink can be more than a little alarming because of one fact: it cannot be erased. The worry caused by potential mistakes is so great for some people that they are put off completely. But what is a mistake? As far as I am concerned, when drawing from life there is no such thing as a mistake.

If one thinks of drawing as a series of approximations, then every mark becomes valuable because it helps in gauging the next. Thus a drawing is built up by an accumulation of marks, each defining a little more the shape being drawn. As the drawing progresses each mark becomes less of an approximation and more of a positive intention. With this approach, each stage of a drawing, including the original statements, is a valuable part of the whole. Therefore there are no 'mistakes'.

With this in mind, it ought to be possible to begin a drawing in ink without any terror of the consequences. Instead, a certain freedom of mind and handling of the pen should prevail. Is it not extraordinary how inhibiting a blank sheet of paper is just before the start of a drawing? It is as if there is some hidden axe waiting to fall as soon as the first 'mistake' occurs. This fear is quite understandable and we all suffer from it to some degree. However, this is precisely where drawing in ink can greatly strengthen your all-round ability.

After a period of using pen and ink I have found that most students' objective eye sharpens up considerably. It assists in overcoming that initial fear of the first statements and helps to obtain an economy of marks based on better observation and also an understanding of the value of line.

As with any other medium, the degree of 'finish' or content will depend upon the length of the pose. For example, short poses of ten to fifteen minutes are ideal

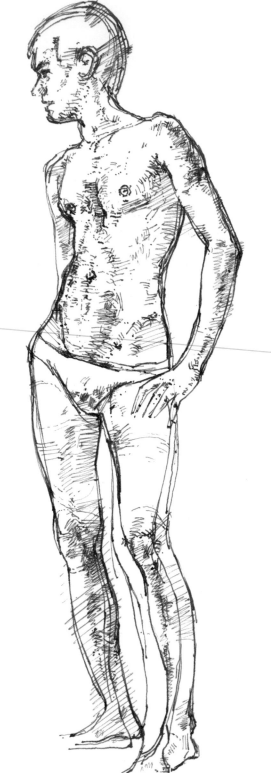

Fig. 49

100

for pen drawing to explore the linear qualities of the pose, but it is equally possible to spend three or four hours on a pen drawing as I have illustrated (**fig. 13**). Be sure, however, when making a long pen drawing, not to sketch it out in pencil first – start with the pen.

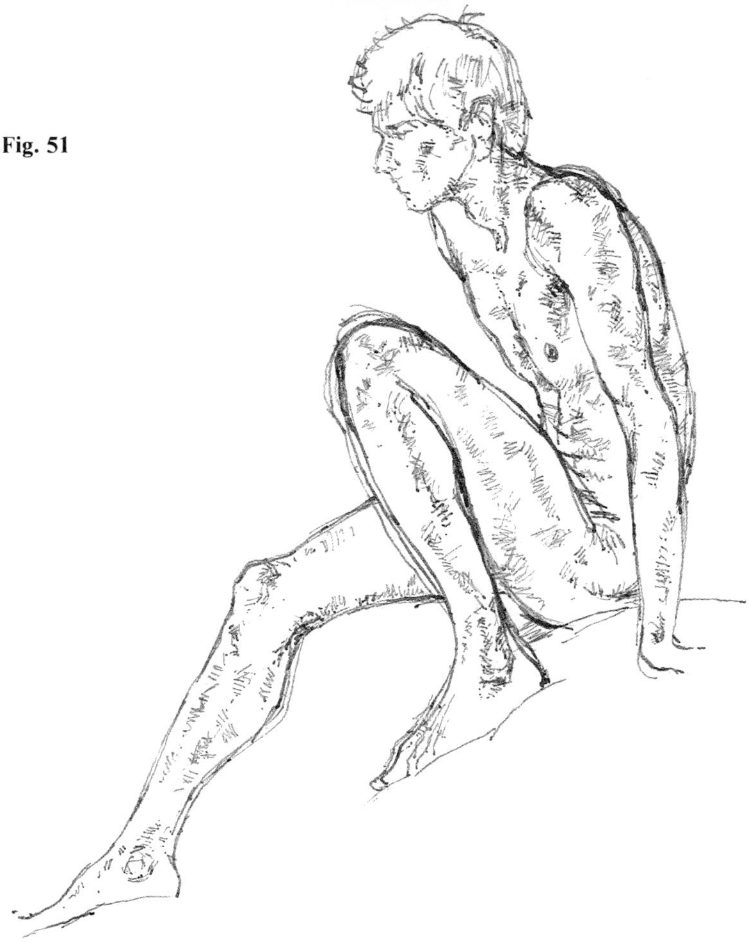

Types of pens

What sort of pen should you use? In the main, a dip pen with a bottle of ink. However, there are many different types of pen that can be used for drawing in ink (see **fig. 3**) and a few of them are mentioned here: steel nib pen with reservoir – the most common type; reed pen – made from a reed, cheap, and with a beautiful touch; quill pen – made from a goose feather which gives it a different feel from the previous two and is very nice to draw with; fountain pen – very convenient, but not to be used with india or any water-proof ink because the shellac content of the ink will cause the pen to clog up (unless, of course, it is a fountain pen made specially for indian ink); Rotring-type – hard, inflexible nib with consistency of thickness of line; biro, felt tips, etc. – useful for drawing, but the ink is impermanent, and they should be used only for sketchbook and not framed drawings.

Fig. 51

Fig. 50

Fig. 52

101

USING PENCIL AND WASH

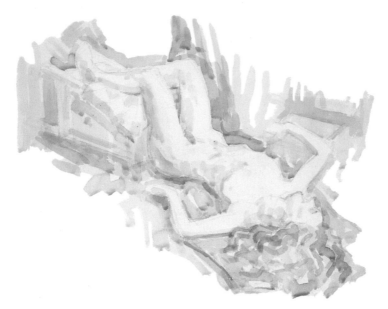

Fig. 53

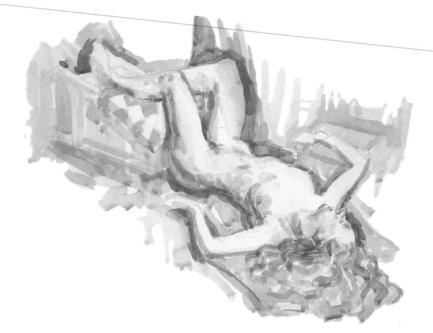

Fig. 54

The purpose of this section is really to demonstrate the possibilities of using wash. Very often wash is used in conjunction with a pen, or in the case of **fig. 55** a pencil, for sharpening up parts of the drawing. I usually prefer a pencil to a pen because I like the neutrality of its colour, and if it is used on wet paper its sensitivity is increased in the same way as chalk (see page 94).

The wash used can either be diluted ink or ordinary watercolour paint. One medium-sized, good-quality brush is all that is needed and as long as it comes to a reasonable point it will suffice for laying a broad wash as well as for more delicate work.

The drawing of the reclining nude in **fig. 53** was begun by broadly indicating with a pencil the constituent parts such as the figure, cushions and stool on its side. As soon as I felt happy with the arrangement, a pale wash was introduced to define where the main tonal areas should be, and also because I wanted the

102

drawing to be constructed with wash rather than by establishing a tightly drawn contour and filling it in.

When making wash drawings I find it very useful to pre-mix three stages of wash – pale, medium and dark. Having used the first wash, laying it everywhere other than direct light-receiving parts, I then move on to the second and finally the third mix. Obviously it is impossible to stick to a very strict order of application because it interferes with the creative spirit. However, by pre-mixing the washes it does at least help to simplify the subject in visual terms.

After the initial wash on the reclining nude in **fig. 53** I began with a darker mix to continue to strengthen the drawing of the figure, not just by working only on the figure but by establishing the tones around it which define more clearly certain shapes. In this instance, the right leg, the forehead and the torso can be seen to be gaining more shape and general status (**fig. 54**). One of the aspects I enjoyed most about this pose was the large amount of hair that flowed away from the body. The brush seemed to be the ideal way in which to treat this network of interesting shapes.

Finally (**fig. 55**), the image as a whole darkens and the character of the pose becomes complete. More background was also worked in to give greater value to the light areas on the figure. Some finer definitions of changes of plane have been added on the torso, but not too strongly or the simple shape of the figure would have been broken up and lost. Halfway through this drawing I took up the pencil and began to define one or two areas more sharply, like the head, right arm and left leg, but the basic character of the drawing is that of wash with broadly defined areas of shape and tone not so easily achieved with pencils or crayons.

Exercise Pose your model in a strong consistent light for three hours. Pre-mix, as described earlier, three stages of wash in separate pans – the colour is immaterial. Using only a very brief pencil sketch, begin to use the wash as soon as possible. Progress through to the final wash, strengthening with a pencil those parts of the drawing you feel are weak. Keep the application of the wash simple and try not to mix too many in-between shades.

Fig. 55

Figs. 53-5 Various stages of a drawing

103

USING WATERCOLOUR

One often sees the term 'watercolour drawing' when it actually refers to a painting. Traditionally, watercolours have often been referred to as drawings, most probably because of their monochromatic use in the eighteenth and nineteenth centuries.

For use in the life room or with any figurative, as opposed to landscape, subject, watercolour is an excellent medium, both convenient to use and capable of great versatility. Although more obviously a painting medium of great subtlety, watercolour can be used to deal with any situation when working from

Fig. 56

Fig. 57

the model for reasonably short periods of time.

I often use watercolour in conjunction with a pencil for sharpening up pieces of drawing at later stages. However, the great value and, indeed, joy of this medium is to use the brush rather than a pencil to begin the drawing. There is a great difference in the feel of a brush compared to pencils or crayons. To draw with a brush forces you to simplify and probably think a great deal harder about the line to be drawn. With pencils and crayons it is very easy to slip into a tentative and sketchy way of drawing, whereas a few sessions with a brush and watercolour can produce some boldly stated but sensitive drawings.

Figs. 56 and 57 were fifteen-minute poses, drawn with just a brush and some dilute colour. **Fig. 57** uses no tone as such, but a series of marks to indicate structure. The actual colour used does not really matter and in fact it is rather a good idea to vary it within the same drawing as you correct or slightly alter lines. The colours of the lines can be varied according to the structure and even the decorative effect of the drawing. As well as depicting lines, the brush is obviously suitable for stating large shadow areas quickly and effectively, and both these operations can be carried out with one good-quality brush, preferably sable, that comes to a decent point.

Sable brushes are of course expensive, but one medium- or large-size brush will not only carry out most functions but will last a lifetime if looked after.

Watercolour boxes come in various sizes ranging from a very tiny pocket size to a large studio type as illustrated in **fig. 4**. Although it is possible to purchase the individual pans of colour and mix them on a separate palette, a box is to be recommended because it holds them all in place and has built-in mixing trays. This makes it compact and easy to use.

Fig. 58
Two-hour drawing

Fig. 59 and Fig. 60 *(below)* Twenty-minute drawings

Fig. **58** was painted as a demonstration for students and I used the bigger box with an additional mixing pan. This was because large areas of wash were used with several overlays during the building up process. The time spent was two hours, sufficient to produce a fairly finished and well-studied work.

The other illustrations in this section, however, were produced from poses of not more than twenty minutes in length. For these I used the small pocket box which can be carried around the whole time and used at a moment's notice. Because the actual amount of watercolour used in these drawings is slight, the area of mixing, in the lid of the box, is quite sufficient.

Fig. **59** has no pencil in it at all and was drawn entirely with a brush. Some colour has been added to emphasize certain shapes. In **fig. 60** the edge of the figure has been created by using the tone of the background, without which the whitish quality of the model's skin would have been lost. **Figs. 61 and 62** were both fifteen-minute poses, the former using pencil and watercolour, the latter brush and watercolour.

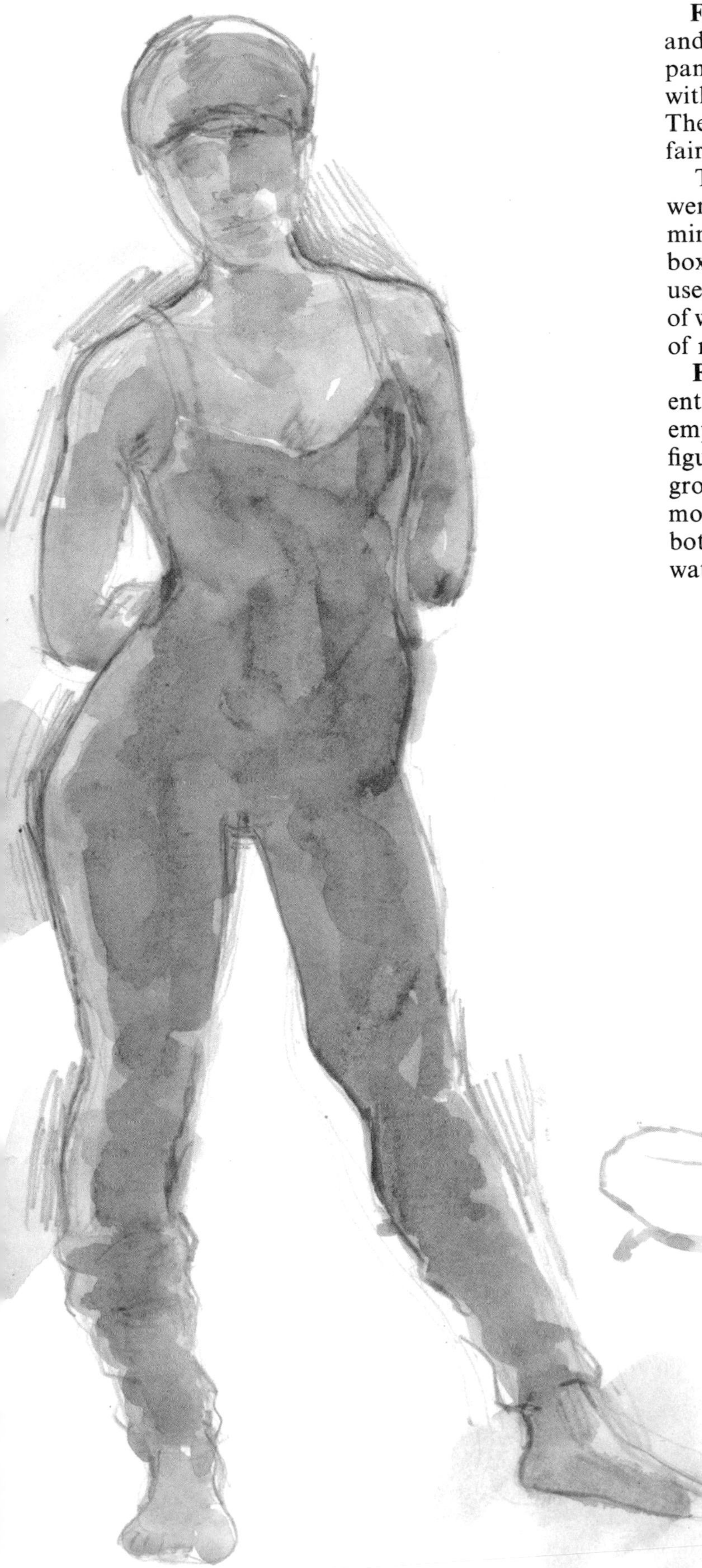

Fig. 61 *(left)*
Fifteen-minute drawing using pencil and watercolour

Fig. 62 *(above)*
Fifteen-minute drawing using brush and watercolour

USING OIL, ACRYLIC AND GOUACHE

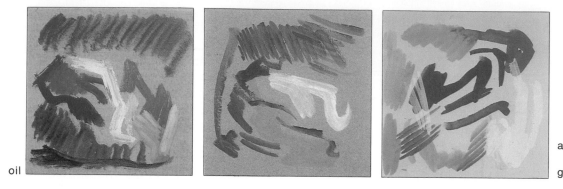

oil

acrylic (centre)

gouache

These three media have one thing in common: they are all opaque paints, whereas watercolour is transparent. The fundamental difference between watercolour and the other three media is the manner in which lighter colours are obtained. Watercolour is diluted with water on white paper, as explained earlier, but oil, acrylic and gouache may all be used in conjunction with white.

It could be said that these media, so obviously used for painting, do not really fit into the practice of drawing too well. This, however, would be to remove a very flexible and powerful means of expression from the artist's repertoire of media for drawing. One only has to think of the use Degas made of oil paint, thinned and used on paper for studies of dancers, to realize its effectiveness.

As anyone who has ever used a brush to draw with knows, there is a very special feeling about it which cannot be achieved by any other method. Drawing with a brush usually involves using the whole arm rather than the wrist and this can produce particularly bold and strong drawings. The tendency is to simplify more than one would do with a pencil and to group areas of contour in a stronger fashion. There is also the possibility of using a full brush to describe tone, shadow or just blocking in.

One of the distinct advantages of these opaque media is the potential use of white either in conjunction with colour or as a way of rectifying drawing. In **fig. 63** (acrylic) the white has been used to increase the silhouette quality of the legs but also to overpaint lines which were not needed. In this way the use of a light colour can be very constructive and not merely decorative.

Just how much colour should be used is a matter of personal judgement. Each artist should be guided by whatever he feels his drawing or study needs to

enhance certain aspects. For the studies of the dancer (**fig. 63**) I used very few colours because I knew that I would not be making a full painting as such but using colour in a more local and descriptive way. The colours used were black, white, red, blue and yellow – the very basic three primaries, plus a lightening and darkening agent. In **figs. 64 and 65** colour has been used to obtain flesh tones, making use of the white to produce various subtle versions of the sorts of pinks and yellows that one sees in flesh. In **fig. 65** (gouache) the colour has also been used to give the study some colour in a more decorative way, in the form of the leg warmers. Without this splash of colour the three figures might have become too large an area of unbroken flesh colours. Notice how in quite a few places the neutral grey of the card has been allowed to show through with only a light application of gouache or none at all.

At this point it might be useful to look at the nature of these media in some detail.

Oil

The usual support for oil painting is canvas or board, but it is quite feasible to use oil paint on card or even paper if it is properly treated. If several sheets of paper are prepared in advance, there should always be a surface available to work on when needed. **Fig. 64** (oil) was painted on cartridge paper, thoroughly sized with two coats of a mixture of cold water and caesin glue, and then toned down to green with acrylic paint. This makes a very acceptable non-greasy surface on which to work. Acrylic can always be used as a primer or underpainting for oil, but never the other way round.

The big disadvantage to using oil paint in a drawing studio is the amount of equipment needed; if the pose is only for an hour or so then obviously one wants to

Fig. 63 Drawing in acrylic

avoid wasting time with turps and squeezing colours out of tubes. Be prepared in advance if this method is to be used.

Acrylic

Acrylic paint is a relatively recent invention and uses a synthetic resin to bind the pigment. It is water-based and is extremely flexible in use, giving thin, water-colour-like washes or thick, opaque mixes like oil paint. It dries within minutes and is thereafter totally waterproof. The advantages over oil are that the support needs no priming or sizing and acrylic can be used direct upon paper with no adverse effects. Being water-based, it is 'cleaner' than oil and there are no

transport problems as it dries immediately. One aspect to beware of, however, is that the colours, once out of the tube, skin and dry quite quickly on both palette and brushes if you are not careful.

Gouache

Although gouache has the opaque properties of the other two media, unlike oil and acrylic it is not water-proof when dry. This, of course, has an effect upon the amount of overpainting possible. The ideal support for gouache is paper or mounting card; I find the centre of window mounts a useful way of using up these leftovers. As with the other two media, gouache is particularly effective on a toned surface, giving the

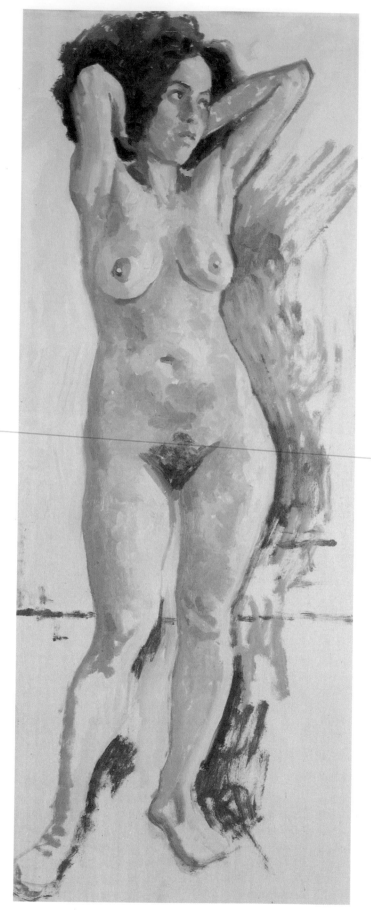

possibility of placing light and dark colours side by side. But one rather distracting feature of gouache is that it has a tendency to change to a different tone when dry, depending on how thick the paint is and how much there is already upon the surface. This can be an irritating aspect of the medium, but one which can easily be dealt with once familiarity is gained.

Should the colours dry on the palette they can be wetted and reused in the same fashion as on a water-colour pan. Gouache, like acrylic, takes only a few minutes to dry and has a very fresh and pastel-like quality.

Fig. 64 *(left)* Drawing in oil

Fig. 65 *(opposite)* Drawing in gouache

110

MIXED MEDIA

So often life drawing is taken as a serious and academic study, which of course it is, but the element of enjoyment and of experimentation should be as strong as possible. Media can play such an important part in any drawing because they can actually affect the whole quality, not so much in the obvious way, but more with regard to the thought process that takes place whilst working. It is for this reason that I feel it is important to try out many different types of media and observe the effect each one has upon both the process and the final outcome of the drawing.

It is equally important to see what happens when media are mixed. There are many reasons why one should want to mix media within one drawing: it could be that from the outset a multi-media effect is sought after; but equally, if not more plausibly, the drawing may demand the introduction of a new medium as it progresses. An example of this might be a drawing begun in red chalk which has reached a stage at which it is no longer possible to make the image any denser because of the colour. At this point it would be useful to introduce black ink to increase the density, and maybe white to highlight some areas

that have become too red. This is a very simple example, but it does illustrate that one way of keeping a drawing going is to change the media each time a passage becomes saturated or overworked.

Fig. 66 was executed in watercolour and coloured pencils. I find the combination of some types of paint and pencil very satisfactory. It is really only when media such as these are combined that texture can be explored. In **fig. 66** the coloured pencil sits very well on top of a watercolour wash in the form of a cross-hatching technique. Alternate layers of wash and crayon were used rather than two single layers. Coloured pencils are about 85 per cent waterproof so when a wash is laid over an area drawn with them the edges may soften slightly, producing a rather attractive effect. If a very sharp and well-defined series of lines is required, coloured pencils should be used last. In this drawing the white paper plays an important part in the luminosity of the body. To try to state something of the pale white, almost porcelain-like quality of the model's skin I felt the delicate overlaying of wash and coloured pencils to be suitable. To emphasize this the striped material was particularly useful.

112

In contrast to this, **fig. 67** was put together with media of far greater covering power. In much the same way as the previous example textures were sought after by combining gouache paint and pastels. Various effects can be achieved, depending upon the stage at which the pastel is introduced. Because the pastel is very soft, by the time it has been applied to the surface it has become virtually pure pigment. This means that if a brush with water, or indeed paint, is put across this the pigment will dissolve and become like a paint. Sometimes this will need quite a lot of pushing around with the brush, depending on the type of pigment. In **fig. 67** some passages of pastel were subsequently dissolved with a brush, but on the whole I was interested in the textures possible by using pastel of a similar colour across an area of gouache.

In both these examples, colour around the figure is important to the final effect. So often insufficient attention is paid to the immediate background of a model, which is a pity because in many cases the only way to achieve something of the pale luminosity of the body is to contrast it against a richly coloured drape or piece of material. Adding background in this way

becomes particularly effective if white paper is used. As mentioned earlier, a toned ground can be very advantageous when adding light colours and it also, of course, provides an immediate background. But in the case of **fig. 67** the drawing was begun on white paper, so a background edge to the figure became rather important.

Fig. 66   *(left)*
Drawing in watercolour and coloured pencils

Fig. 67   *(above)* Drawing in gouache and pastels

ANATOMY FOR THE ARTIST

Fig. 68

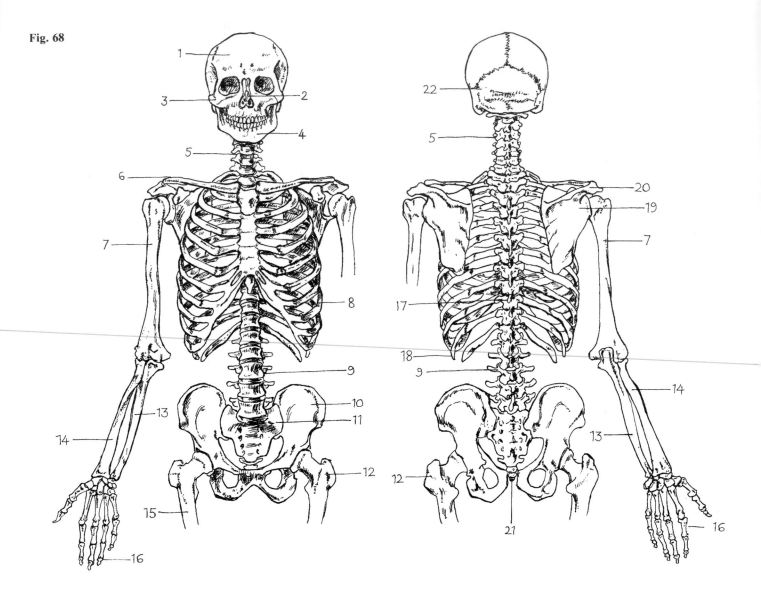

As the majority of this book is concerned with working from a nude figure it seems appropriate to include a brief survey of the anatomy of the human figure. It is a complex and involved subject and can be studied to whatever degree the artist concerned feels is necessary. Here I shall aim to give only an introduction and basic information on the bones and muscles.

Is a knowledge of anatomy essential to becoming a good figurative artist? Not necessarily, because a good draughtsman can cope with any situation; but undoubtedly it can be useful and will enhance any drawing made from life. Very often drawing problems which seem insoluble when working from a model can be reasoned out far better with a little knowledge of

Fig. 68 Bones of the head, thorax and arm

1 Frontal bone
2 Nasal bone
3 Zygomatic arch
4 Mandible
5 Cervical vertebrae (7)
6 Clavicle
7 Humerus
8 Rib cage
9 Lumbar vertebrae (5)
10 Iliac bone
11 Sacrum
12 Great trochanter of femur
13 Ulna
14 Radius
15 Femur
16 Bones of the hand
17 Dorsal vertebrae (12)
18 Floating ribs (2 pairs)
19 Scapula
20 Acromion
21 Coccyx
22 Occipital

anatomy. If an artist were asked to make a drawing of a boat, provided his objective faculties were good, he should be reasonably successful. However, if he happened to have an intimate knowledge about the construction of sailing vessels, the drawing would have a greater certainty about it, for if at any time there was confusion about technical details he, with his knowledge of boats, would probably make a drawing with more conviction.

Of course, as with all objective drawing, you should always draw what you see rather than what you know. In this way a basic knowledge of anatomy can be an invaluable aid to objective drawing.

Fig. 69 Bones of the leg and foot
1	Femur	**8**	Sacrum
2	Patella	**9**	Navicular
3	Tibia	**10**	Calcaneus
4	Fibula	**11**	Cuboid
5	Talus	**12**	Bones of the foot
6	Great trochanter of femur		
7	Pelvis		

Fig. 69

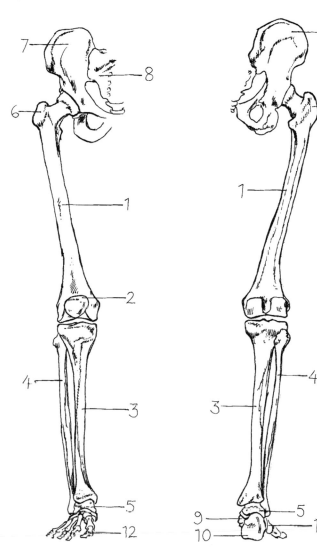

The skeleton

To begin our survey of human anatomy let us consider the skeleton (see **figs. 68 and 69**), the armature or frame upon which everything else rests. The skeleton has evolved to give maximum mobility and stability to the movements we perform. The spine forms the central part of the structure, supporting the skull and twelve pairs of ribs. These provide the cover and protection for the lungs and internal organs. When it reaches the pelvis the spine rests and divides the body weight evenly on to the legs. This creates great stability, yet allows many complex movements from the waist upwards while keeping the feet firmly planted on the ground.

The pelvis is the part of the skeleton which shows the greatest difference between the sexes. In the female it is wider and shallower, with a much greater distance between the coccyx and the pubic arch, which, of course, has its effect upon the superficial form with the characteristic wider hips in women. It is always important to study this area in standing poses and it is essential to get the correct angle across the hips.

The weight from the thorax, spread across the pelvis, is then transmitted on to the two femur bones. The femur is the longest and strongest bone in the whole body and connects to the pelvis by means of a ball and socket joint. This, compared to the similar joint at the scapula and humerus, is much deeper for greater stability, whereas the shoulder junction is shallower for increased mobility.

The junction at the knee consists of the femur resting on top of the tibia, upon which there are two shallow depressions with the corresponding condyles at the base of the femur. At the front, connected by ligaments only, is a small bone called the patella. This joint, of course, can only move backwards and forwards as far as the front line of the leg. Connected to the outside of the tibia is the fibula, which at the lower end forms the ankle.

The bones of the foot comprise seven tarsals, five metatarsals and three phalanges for each toe except the big toe, which has only two.

Returning to the upper skeleton, the shoulders are formed by the clavicle in the front and the acromion of the scapula at the back. This is the other area of the skeleton where a marked difference between the sexes occurs, male shoulders being generally wider than females'.

The arms and hands perform the most complex movements of the body, and this is due entirely to their structure. From the scapula, connected by a shallow ball and socket joint, is the humerus, which at the opposite end forms a joint for two bones, the radius and ulna. As the name implies, the radius crosses the

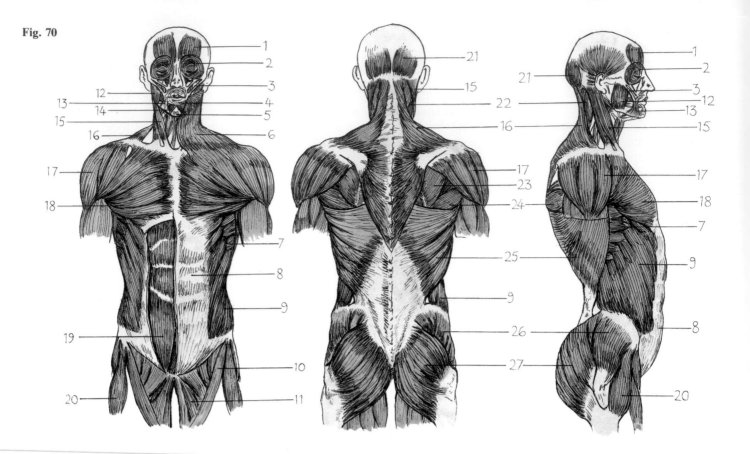

Fig. 70

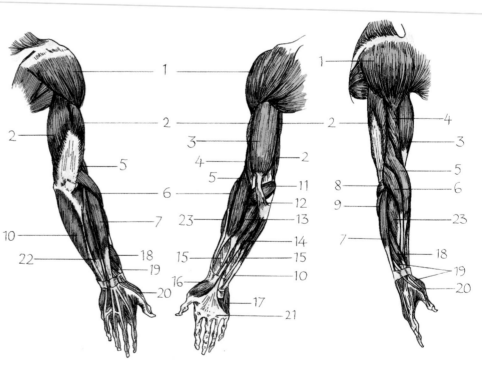

Fig. 70 Muscles of the head, neck and trunk

1 Frontalis
2 Orbicularis of the eye
3 Zygomaticus major and minor
4 Orbicularis of the mouth
5 Mentalis
6 Platysma
7 Serratus anterior
8 Aponeurosis covering the rectus abdominis
9 External oblique
10 Sartorius
11 Adductor longus
12 Masseter
13 Depressor of the angle of the mouth
14 Elevator of the chin
15 Sternomastoid
16 Trapezius
17 Deltoid
18 Pectoralis major
19 Rectus abdominis
20 Tensor fasciae latae
21 Occipitalis
22 Splenius capitis
23 Infraspinatus
24 Teres major
25 Latissimus dorsi
26 Gluteus medius
27 Gluteus maximus

Fig. 71

Fig. 72

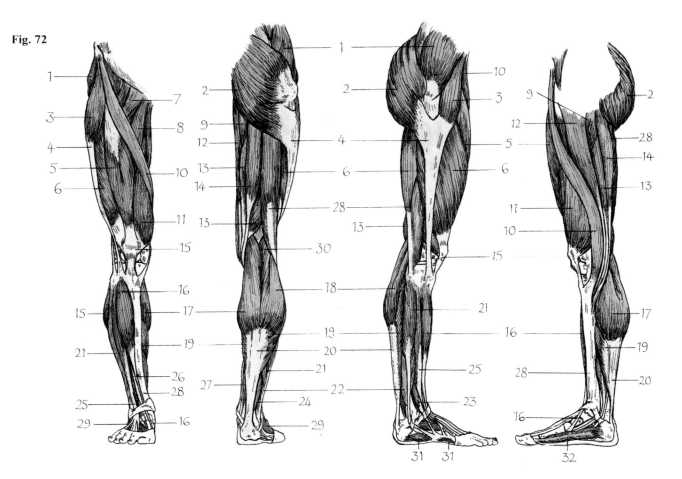

ulna, taking with it all the bones of the wrist and the hand.

There are many small bones which form the wrist and, like the foot, the hand comprises five bones called metacarpals and three phalanxes for each finger except the thumb, which has two.

Muscles

Within this survey of the anatomy of the human body there is not room to discuss each muscle and its movements at length. However, it would be useful to mention the main groups (see **figs. 70-72**) and their functions as they affect us as draughtsmen.

What can actually be seen on the surface of a body, of course, is often rather limited and depends on whether the individual has an athletic form or is overweight. In all cases the muscular form never appears on the surface exactly as it really is. Even in the thinnest people there is a layer of fatty tissue, known as the panniculus adiposus, covering the entire body. In addition, muscles combine to work in groups so that on the surface, and especially by the time they have been covered by skin and fat, it is not always possible to trace the effect of an individual muscle. However, what is of great value and assistance to an artist is a knowledge of the underlying structure of a figure, which will help him to draw with more understanding.

There are roughly two types of muscle in the body: those which are long and small in width but often thick, occurring in the arms and legs; and wide sheet-like muscles which are found in the torso. Joining the head to the shoulders is a very important muscle called the sternomastoid, and this is always visible. It connects just behind the ear and runs diagonally to the clavicle (collar bone) to form the pit of the neck. At the back, the upper part of the trapezius connects to the rear of the cranium.

The muscles of the torso are more like cladding and provide protection for the important internal organs. At the front of the torso is a large muscle which connects the rib cage to the pelvis and is used in such movements as pulling the torso towards the legs as in the 'sit up' exercise. This is called the rectus abdominis and can always be seen to good effect on the surface despite the fact that it often carries some fat.

To the side of the torso the two main muscles are the external oblique and serratus anterior. The serratus connects to the scapula and assists in certain arm movements and is sometimes called the fencer's muscle.

At the back, running from the cervical vertebrae connecting to the dorsal and lumbar vertebrae, is a group of deep-lying muscles called erector spinae, which give the back its characteristic 'furrow' in the centre (see **fig. 73**). Lying over this group are the superficial muscles of the back, latissimus dorsi and trapezius. Both these muscles are broad, thin and cover large areas. The latissimus dorsi muscle covers virtually the whole back and comes round to the front to form the armpit along with pectoralis major, the muscle of the chest.

Fig. 73

Fig. 73 Deep muscles of the back
1 Splenius capitis
2 Levator scapulae
3 Rhomboideus
4 Erector spinae
5 Serratus posterior

Fig. 74 Muscles of the arm
1 Deltoid
2 Triceps
3 Biceps
4 Extensor digitorum
5 Extensor carpi radialis longus

6 Ulna
7 Radius
8 Extensor carpi ulnaris

Fig. 75 Muscles of the leg
1 Tensor fasciae latae
2 Biceps femoris
3 Soleus
4 Peroneus longus
5 Tibialis anterior
6 Vastus lateralis
7 Achilles tendon
8 Gastrocnemius

Fig. 74

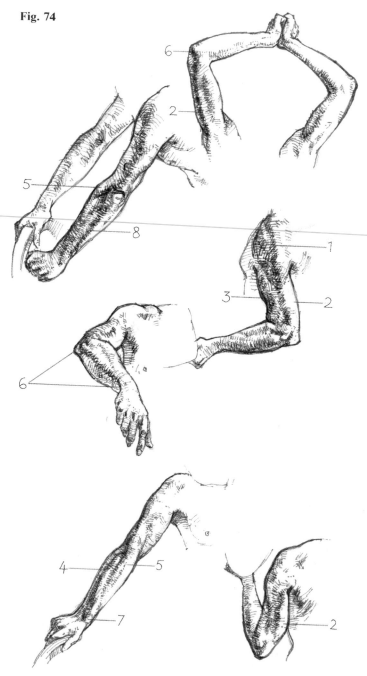

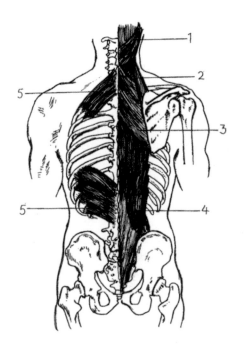

118

To form the connection to the arm the other important muscle in this area is the deltoid, so called because of its resemblance to the Greek letter Δ (delta). This is a powerful muscle which governs most of the whole-arm movements. The muscles which clad the humerus bone are few, but strong. The main two are the biceps and triceps, which both connect to the scapula and then to the radius and ulna respectively. These muscles are responsible for many of the movements of the forearm.

The character of the muscles of the lower arm is rather different. Here there are many long, thin muscles which connect by tendons to the fingers and thumb. The characteristic shape of the forearm is achieved because at the fleshy end of the muscles they combine to produce a bulky shape before tapering into thin tendons at the wrist. Of this group of muscles there are two which are rather more powerful than the others and which connect to the humerus, the forearm being lifted by their crane-like action. These are the brachioradialis and extensor carpi radialis longus.

The muscles of the leg resemble those of the arm to some degree. In the upper portion they are thicker and stronger for moving the entire limb, and below the knee they are thinner and result in numerous tendons which connect to and move the toes. At the back and at the top the powerful gluteus maximus forms the main muscle of the buttock and is used for running and leaping. This area, more than any other, is prone to accumulating fat and the actual muscles can really only be seen properly on an athletic person.

Connecting to the lower part of the pelvis and running the whole length of the femur is a group of muscles which form the 'hamstrings' as they part over

Fig. 75

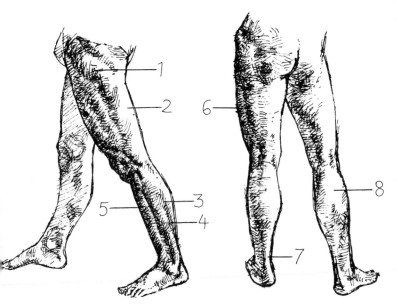

the calf. This is an area of common tendon where several muscles join at the same point. At the front upper portion the sartorius runs from the outer edge of the pelvis diagonally across the leg to join the hamstring, and this muscle, although not always visible in its entirety, forms the basic character of the upper leg. It is very important to artists, for its effect on the overall shape of the upper leg is always apparent. Another area of common tendon is the joining of the gluteus maximus, gluteus medius and tensor fasciae latae, to form the ilio tibial band.

The area known as the calf consists of a muscle called the gastrocnemius which is divided into two portions. These connect to the femur and in conjunction with the hamstrings, which connect below the knee to the tibia and fibula, form a powerful junction which operates the whole of the lower leg. At the opposite end the gastrocnemius becomes a tendon which, as it approaches the foot, forms the familiar Achilles tendon. This attaches to the calcaneus bone and performs many of the main movements of the foot.

At the front of the lower leg the tibia bone lies just under the surface of the skin and thin fatty tissue. This is one of the few areas on the body where bone can be observed only just under the surface, the others being the collar bone (clavicle) and the iliac crest of the pelvis. To the outside of the lower leg is the peroneal group of muscles which contribute to movements of the foot.

Like the hand, the foot has very little fleshy content and comprises mainly bones and those tendons which attach to them. These tendons, as in the forearm, are the tapered ends of muscles which when grouped form the bulky area of the calf.

All muscles have a fleshy part, which expands and contracts depending on the signal from the brain. This fleshy part is then joined to a tendon, which does the pulling or pushing. In the diagrams of muscles I have coloured the fleshy parts red and the tendons yellow. The following short list explains the movements of the muscles as implied by their name:

Abduction This describes the movement away from the central axis of the body; an example of this would be lifting the arm or leg upwards and outwards.

Adduction This is the opposite of abduction and describes the movement of a limb back towards the central axis of the body or even beyond it.

Extensor A muscle which, when contracted, will extend or straighten a joint.

Flexor The opposite of extensor. When contraction occurs it brings together the two parts it connects; for example, 'flexing the biceps'.

119

HEADS, HANDS AND FEET

Fig. 76 *(left)* Chalk drawing

Fig. 77 *(above)* Drawing in coloured pencils

These are the parts of the body which most people seem to have difficulty drawing. In theory, there is no reason why hands and feet should be any more difficult to draw than any other part of the body, although a special case could be made concerning the head in relation to portrait drawing and painting. If included as part of a general figure drawing, none of these extremities should really have too much attention paid to them. When the scale of a drawing is quite small, much simplification of the head and hands is needed in particular.

However, the extremities are of obvious interest because, in the case of the head and hands, these parts of the body contain much of the individual character of a person and therefore merit some special attention. There are, of course, no formulas for dealing with any aspect of drawing, but there are some points which one can bear in mind whilst drawing.

Fig. 76 shows a chalk drawing of an elderly man. The face has plenty of character, absorbed over a life-time, and makes an obviously attractive subject. For such a study, placing the head in a good light and in a position that is sympathetic to your aim is important. In the case of an older person, it is not advisable to get too involved with wrinkles because it can give the effect of a screwed-up cloth. Overall shape, structure and proportion are important; observe, for instance, the distance from the top of the head to the eyebrow, the length of the nose and the length from the nose to the chin. The angles of the eyebrows, ear and moustache can also give great indication of the character of the model.

Compare this to **fig. 77** of a young girl. Generally speaking, the form is much smoother and tighter on a young person, which makes the changes of plane very subtle. Here the model's hair plays a very

Fig. 78

Fig. 80

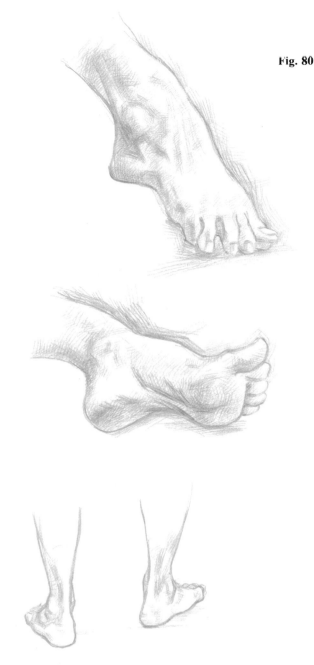

Fig. 79

important part in the shape and overall character of the head. Never forget that hair, regardless of how much there is, is a vital part of a portrait head. So often I have seen student drawings of 'faces' that appear to be no more than a mask because no consideration has been paid to the hair. When one looks at cartoons of famous people very often they are identifiable by the hairstyle alone. Sometimes, however, as in this drawing, hair can obscure vital pieces of information, such as the eyes, but this is a challenge which must be met. The hair covering the face of this girl is as important to her character as the lack of it is to the elderly gentleman.

Because hands are in constant use and perform a vast range of movements, it would seem natural, when making a detailed study, to draw hands employed in some activity. Hands differ greatly between individuals, depending upon age and occupation, so with any comprehensive study it would be advantageous to include a cross section. **Fig. 78** shows a pair of male hands performing the ordinary task of hammering. Observe how the right hand gripping the hammer has veins and knuckles quite well defined and makes an interesting pattern of shadow areas. The hands holding the pot (**fig. 79**) make a good study because of their relationship to each other in performing the task. Notice the position of the fingers in relation to the thumb and how on the left hand the rim of the pot causes the little finger to adopt an unusual angle.

Finally, the feet illustrated in **fig. 80** show just how interesting they can be in close-up. Because there is so little flesh on them, the bone and tendons are very near to the surface, and every movement has a significant effect upon the superficial form. Notice how the ankle is higher on the inside (tibia bone) than outside (fibula bone) in the drawing of the rear view of two feet.

MOVEMENT IN DRAWING

Fig. 81
Group of ink drawings made at an exercise class

Fig. 82
Drawing in charcoal

Earlier on I discussed the merits of drawing shorter-length poses as they often contain certain expressive elements that longer poses do not. To go one stage further, where the model is not posing at all, can be very exciting indeed. By this I mean drawing figures in movement.

The great value of drawing a moving figure – a dancer, for example – is that, unlike with a posed model, it is possible to follow a movement through and attempt to understand how the body works in these situations. Obviously the nature of the actual drawing has to change to suit the conditions. When drawing a posed model the usual procedure is to look repeatedly at the model before making each mark, perhaps every four or five seconds. When drawing a moving figure, however, it is more a question of studying the movement intensely and then working swiftly from the visual memory until the vision fades. Instead of trying to describe the various parts of the body accurately it is probably more useful to aim for a drawing that expresses the movement as a whole.

Fig. 81 shows a group of drawings I made at an exercise workout class; each individual drawing took between one and two minutes to do. Classes such as these and dance classes are ideal places to draw because the costumes worn are skintight and show the bodily characters well, and movements or exercises are generally repeated several times making it possible to understand in more detail their nature.

My drawings were made in ink – a fountain pen with drawing ink, which I find very convenient for this sort of an occasion. Although almost any medium can be used for this, the obvious advantage of ink is that you get an immediate and non-erasable image which is very important when the actual drawing time is measured in seconds. Large amounts of paper or an

empty sketchbook are also needed because once momentum is gained drawings can pour out at a prolific rate.

At the end of a session it is good to lay out all your drawings on to the floor, select a handful of the most successful ones and perhaps mount them on a single sheet as in **fig. 81**. Out of thirty or forty quick drawings you may find that only half a dozen work well, but this does not mean the others are failures; on the contrary, they would have been an essential part of the process without which the good half dozen would not have been possible.

Fig. 82 is a charcoal drawing made from swift notations, like the composite illustration (**fig. 81**). Using the information gained on the spot, I put this drawing together, in the studio, with the aim of taking the movement theme a stage further into composition and design. The positions of the arms and legs are vital to the flow of the movement from one figure to another.

In **figs. 83 and 84** the same idea has been used, but this time with the addition of colour in the form of gouache and pastels. Up to this point the drawings show almost a pure linear method of description, but with the introduction of colour comes tone and silhouette quality. The composition can now be further enhanced by using a near silhouette in places where the dancers are wearing black costumes.

Exercise If it is not possible to gain access to a dance class, ask your model to wear a leotard or similar outfit suitable for exercising. Then arrange for a series of movements to be repeated and make drawings which capture the whole movement. When enough drawings have been made in this fashion, use them to make a composition, taking the movement theme further as illustrated in **fig. 82**.

Fig. 83 *(left)* and Fig. 84 *(below)* Drawings in charcoal, gouache and pastels

CLOTHED FIGURES

Fig. 85
Identical poses: one unclothed, one clothed

Fig. 86
Drawing in carbon pencil

Perhaps in the same way that anatomy can assist the knowledge of the superficial human form, so life drawing itself will obviously help a great deal in understanding the shape of a figure in clothes. Whatever the shape of the clothes there will always be points at which the form underneath can be observed, as the article of clothing is stressed across it. **Fig. 85** shows a figure in two identical poses: one clothed and one unclothed. The hips and shoulders are obvious points from which the clothes can be seen to hang. Notice, too, how the sleeve of the blouse behaves on the extended arm; gravity causes the material to hang so the top edge of the arm shows the form underneath quite well.

Fig. 86 is a fairly straightforward pencil drawing made in a linear way to depict the effect of folds upon a suit. Because of the position the man is standing in, some parts of his clothing display many creases whereas those areas where no significant bending takes place are relatively crease-free. A suit such as this is carefully designed and tailored to achieve a certain effect which is complementary to the body inside it. It also possesses well-thought-out proportions; for instance, the way in which the waistcoat appears to finish fairly high and overlaps the trousers, thus making the legs appear to be longer than perhaps they really are.

This contrasts rather nicely with **fig. 88**, which depicts somebody wearing fairly loose-fitting clothing.

Rather than looking for individual folds in this drawing, I sought a more overall effect about the figure as a whole. It seemed important to try to state something of the character of the model in her clothes.

Fig. 88 was made as a preliminary to a life drawing session. Very often it can be advantageous to draw your model with clothes on before beginning or even after finishing a life drawing. If it is a model you are familiar with, this can be of great benefit in getting to understand how clothes work upon a person.

Exercise Make a drawing from a pose of one and a half to two hours and then ask your model to put his or her clothes back on and take up exactly the same position. Note where the stress points come and compare your second drawing with your first.

Fig. 88
Drawing in pen and wash

Fig. 87
Drawing in ink

126

FIGURES
IN AN ENVIRONMENT

Fig. 89 Drawing in watercolour and pencil

Most of this book has been concerned with studies of single figures in one form or another. When some experience has been gained with figure drawing, the obvious progression is into making a composition including several figures. These would then have to be seen in some sort of environment. In various sections of the book I have stressed the need to relate the figure to its immediate background, even if it is only a tone without any description. When figures are put into an environment, this obviously becomes essential; you will appreciate then having already done this from time to time in the life room.

Lighting is important, of course, because the source of light always has a great effect upon any interior.

Fig. 89 is one of a series of watercolour and pencil studies I did in preparation for a large oil painting. With four figures to set into a large room I felt the need to experiment with various combinations of sitting and standing poses. When making studies of this sort one becomes particularly aware of how people behave when they are sitting or standing and whether they are comfortable and relaxed or ill at ease with their immediate surroundings. The lady on the sofa seemed to be rightly posed from the beginning whereas I placed the other three differently in other studies to see the effect.

The other important factor in a study of this sort is the space that surrounds the figures and the effect it

has upon them. Unlike life drawings where one auto-matically 'closes up' on the subject, here various effects can be achieved, depending upon how far away the subject is placed.

Fig. 90, in watercolour, shows a girl in a pose reminiscent of many seen in a life drawing studio. In this instance she was placed in the fairly natural surroundings of an attic bedroom, and as always the lighting is of the utmost importance. Rather than going for a particularly accurate or anatomically descriptive figure, I thought it important that the model should take her place within the scheme of the whole interior and the lighting effect. Thus the side of her nearest the window is rather well defined and the opposite side is much closer in tone to the background with less contrast.

Because of the vertical nature of the pose it is also most important to place the figure sympathetically within the rectangle. Here she relates to the other two verticals of the window area, creating an interesting division and proportional arrangement. Although the architecture of an interior may seem impossible to alter, remember that a figure is a more flexible agent and can be moved around more easily when working out compositions of this nature.

Fig. 90   Drawing in watercolour